Is Democracy Possible?

Is Democracy Possible?

The alternative to electoral politics

JOHN BURNHEIM

University of California Press

Berkeley   Los Angeles

©John Burnheim, 1985

1985

First published in the United States by
University of California Press
Berkeley and Los Angeles, California

Library of Congress Catalog Number 85-40664

ISBN 0-520- 05662-0

Printed in Great Britain

Contents

Preface

The ideas in this book were originally expressed in the context of a philosophical manuscript in 1979, and in two different articles entitled 'Statistical Democracy', one in *Radical Philosophy*, no. 27, Spring 1981 and the other in *Thesis Eleven* no. 3, 1981, p. 60. Since then a number of people have read one or other essay and various drafts of the present book. Noam Chomsky, Ferenc Feher and C. B. Macpherson offered valuable encouragement. Carole Pateman read a late version of the present book and offered helpful suggestions, as did Graham Nerlich, Geoffrey Blunden, Wal Suchting and Barry Hindess, who suggested the publisher to me.

More generally, I am grateful to my colleagues and students in the Department of General Philosophy for forcing me to think critically and practically about the problems of democracy and of social decision-making. My deepest and most comprehensive debt is to Wal Suchting. Gyorgy Markus has contributed a great deal, not least his critique of 'actually existing socialism' in *Dictatorship over Needs* (Oxford, Basil Blackwell: 1983), with Ferenc Feher and Agnes Heller.

Pat Bower and Charle Reimer were responsible for typing innumerable drafts. The staff at Polity Press and at Basil Blackwell have been most helpful, especially Anthony Giddens, Helen Pilgrim and Pat Lawrence.

Finally, my wife, Margaret Harris, and children, Catherine and Lucy, had to put up with numerous ill-effects of my preoccupation with this book. To them it is gratefully and affectionately dedicated.

John Burnheim Sydney, January 1985.

Introduction

I A FIRST APPROACH TO THE ISSUES

Democracy does not exist in practice. At best we have what the ancients would have called elective oligarchies with strong monarchical elements. Most contemporary discussions of democracy assume that the task of democratic theory is to provide either some justification for these regimes or some normative guidance for their improvement.[1] It is assumed that the state is a necessity of social life. The question is whether it can be made more democratic. One of my aims is to disprove this assumption by showing how a polity might function without the centralization of government that constitutes the state. There is no denying that social life is impossible without government. There must be decision-making bodies that exercise coercive power over groups and individuals. Moreover, the decisions of governing bodies must be co-ordinated, and where negotiation fails some co-ordinating decision must be imposed on them if peace and rationality are to prevail. But this neither necessitates nor justifies any body possessing a *monopoly* of power to decide and enforce decisions about matters of public and common concern.

For a variety of reasons I begin with practicalities, though of a very general and abstract sort, rather than with a theory of human nature or of society or of rights and authority. Discussions of these latter matters always involve assumptions about what can be done or is likely to happen. The values we emphasize reflect our hopes and fears and the experience from which these spring. The very concepts we use in political theory are bound up with the structuring of our social world by specific social practices. What human nature is is a matter of what human beings can do. And what they can do is a matter of what they have ways of doing, individually and collectively. What rights seem necessary for people to enjoy and what authority is desirable are a function of needs that take definite shape only in definite forms of social life. No doubt human nature is neither indefinitely plastic nor perfectible, but equally certainly what human beings can do remains a matter to be explored. There is no well-founded theoretical basis on which arguments about human nature can resolve our present problems. It is, I hope to show, both more profitable and more honest to address ourselves explicitly to practical problems and their solution in the first instance. Here the constraints are quite specific. Nevertheless, the solution is unlikely to arise simply from the analysis of the problem. It will call for philosophical reflection about its desirability as well as for argument for its practicability. In the long run, however, proposals can be tested only in political practice, which will judge both their feasibility and desirability.

The main practical problem about democracy is easily stated: in any full-blooded sense 'government of the people, by the people, for the people' seems impossible in any but the narrowest range of circumstances. For government by the people to occur the people must make the decisions that constitute the content of government. But there is no way in which they can make these decisions, much less make them on a sound basis, when the decisions involve so many people in so many different ways as do the decisions involved in legislating and administering in a modern state. This is not a matter of technical difficulties of communication. Today we can organize and address assemblies hundreds of times as big as the Greeks could. It would be possible to provide everybody with the means of listening to debates on any topic and recording a vote on every issue without their leaving their

armchairs. But people would be reduced to accepting or rejecting proposals. There is no way in which any significant proportion could participate in framing them. Aristotle and
other ancient critics of democracy argued that it inevitably
degenerated into rule by the orators and ultimately into
tyranny. The bigger and more passive the audience the more
that is likely to happen.

Moreover, if the point of democracy is that good decisions,
decisions that reflect the long-term interests of the people,
should be made, it is questionable whether people can know
enough to make rational decisions on the very large range of
issues that have to be faced. This point has nothing to do with
the 'ignorance of the mob'. It applies equally well to professional politicians, social scientists or any other aristocracy. It
is an argument against all centralization of decision-making
power whether in an individual, a small group or a mass
assembly. Clearly the force of the difficulty is a function both
of the size and complexity of a society and of the degree to
which its affairs are ordered by explicit administrative decisions, its degree of socialism. Advocates of the market
mechanism have used it as an argument for small government
and advocates of certain kinds of socialism have insisted on it
as an argument for small autonomous communities. I shall
argue that both of these solutions to the problem are unsatisfactory.

Again, there are inherent difficulties in the vague concept
of 'the people'. For all those who, from Plato and Aristotle
onwards, have accepted the importance of class power in
politics, rule by the people comes down in practice to rule of
the poor over the rich. As long as the economic system functions to produce control of the means of production by a few,
class differences will persist. The attempt of the 'have-nots'
to use the power of government to limit the power of those
who control the means of production must always lead to
a situation of self-defeating conflict, If a market or, more
specifically, a capitalist system is to flourish it must be possible

for owners of capital to make long-term investments with a reasonable probability of profit. Attempts to redistribute income by taxation must either fail to have any substantial effect or result in lack of investment and economic hardship for those in need of employment. Instability produces war and repression. Ruling groups that are threatened by popular power have always been inclined to use military means, demagogy and treachery to protect their interests. Only in a classless society does the notion of the people acquire a genuinely inclusive extension. In a class society its oscillates between a more general and a more specific meaning in a way that reflects the contradictory interests of the different classes. But is a genuinely classless society possible? Is it possible to avert concentrations of *economic* power and of status only at the cost of an intolerably restrictive concentration of *political* power in the hands of those who claim to represent the people?

Moreover, the concept of the people covers up an enormous variety of differences of interest connected with specific forms of life and community property. Most significantly, each nation-state treats its own territory as a collective property subject to no external interference. The people are always the French or British or Guatemalan people. 'The people of the world' has a hollow ring even in rhetorical contexts. It corresponds to no operative reality. But many of the problems that we face, ecological, economic and humane, are soluble only on a global basis and with an eye to the future needs of all humankind. If government by the people for the people can be conceived coherently only as government by all existing human beings in the long-term interests of the human race and of the world that it dominates, it is not patently impossible? Would any nation be willing to submit itself to a world state that would dictate to it how its resources were to be used and disrupt its way of life to conform to the prescriptions of some remote majority? How could such a remote and all-powerful body admit of any meaningful participation by the thousands of millions whom it governed? Can there be world democracy without a world state?

There is, finally, a fundamental point of principle that is hardly ever addressed by democratic theorists. It is desirable that each person or group should have an opportunity for influencing decisions of any matter in direct proportion to their legitimate material interest in the outcome. It is not often noticed that this principle is ineffectual unless its converse is also satisfied. *Nobody should have any input into decision-making where they have no legitimate material interest.* The notion of legitimate material interest calls for explication. Roughly, by 'material' I mean to exclude interests that people have simply because of their intrusive desires about how others should fare, while by 'legitimate' I mean to exclude material interests that are not based on entitlements that are morally sound.

The point of these exclusions is obvious enough. Individuals or groups do not acquire the sort of interest that entitles them to have a say in determining what I or some group to which I belong may do simply by their having strong feelings about the matter. Their interest must have a more material ground than their thinking about the matter. Equally, people may have good reason to covet things that I am entitled to, but that does not give them a legitimate interest in those things. In particular, in regard to public goods there is often a serious confusion between people's legitimate material interest in the opportunity costs of providing some good for a particular group and their unwarranted claims to determine just what is good for the group in question. There may be a reasonable argument that the money should have been spent elsewhere. But if it is allocated to a certain educational programme, for example, the precise form that programme should take is a matter on which those who are directly affected by it should normally decide.

If these principles are not observed the result is tyranny, perhaps well-intentioned or unobtrusive tyranny, but tyranny in a strict sense. People are exercising authority over others, without warrant and without regard to their proper autonomy, by virtue of possessing political power.

All present forms of democracy and all hitherto proposed forms of it not only permit but encourage such tyranny. The result is that they strain their claims to be called democracy and their claims to superiority over monarchies and oligarchies. Normally they become oligarchies that are defensible only on the grounds that no better alternative is available.

That this degeneration is a normal consequence of everybody having a say in everything is not difficult to understand. In a very small and amicable group people may abstain from using their votes on matters that do not concern them on the basis of a convention that it is the proper thing to do. The convention may be sustained by interpersonal relationships. In larger groups it tends to break down. Vote-trading becomes the key to success. Not to use every opportunity to extract the maximum return for one's agreement to vote in a certain way is to invite defeat at the hands of those who do. The more uninterested one is in the specific issues the better. It makes it so much easier to trade favours uninhibitedly. Naturally, one may need to put some sort of face on it, but usually that of a soundly pragmatic man will do.

What happens in this process is utterly different from what happens in a genuine exchange of substantive interests. If each of us quite legitimately has some title to the same thing we shall have to bargain about what each is willing to trade for the other's title, or perhaps submit to arbitration or the toss of a coin. Each of us has some power over the other, but unless one of us is so poor in entitlements as not to be able to secure any reasonable set of his or her interests, or is in particularly desperate need of just this thing, the exchange will normally be fair. The exchange ceases to be fair when what I get in exchange for my substantive good is merely release from an arbitrary threat on your part. The obvious case arises when you threaten to harm me physically unless I hand over what you want. But any threat to use arbitrarily power that you have to harm me without substantive cost to yourself is equally obnoxious, whether it is done out of malice or self-interest, or even paternalism.

Now in any present form of democracy it is quite usual for it to be necessary to buy the votes of many people who have no legitimate material interest in the matter in hand in order to meet the interests of those who do have a genuine interest in it. Electoral democracy carries this to the point where the 'numbers-men', the power brokers, operating through political parties and professionally organized lobbies, manipulate these disposable votes into concentrations of power for their own aggrandizement. The trick is to buy people's votes over the whole range of matters that come up for decision on the basis of committing oneself to some limited set of promises about the few things that they feel strongly about. To make matters worse, those strong feelings are often not based on legitimate material interests. The system is corrupt and corrupting. We do not realize how badly it functions only because the existing alternatives are worse.

II   FUNCTIONAL AUTONOMY

Our task is to disentangle the knot of assumptions that go to make these difficulties; rejecting some, showing how others can be dealt with, accepting others. At the risk of being dismissed out of hand, I shall indicate what my strategy is. I shall argue that most of the decisions that are now taken by centrally controlled multi-function agencies ranging from nation-states down to municipalities could be taken by autonomus specialized agencies that are co-ordinated by negotiation among themselves or, if that fails, by quasi-judicial arbitration, rather than by direction from a controlling body. Participation in the decision-making process in each body should extend not to 'the people' generally, but to those who are affected by the decisions in question to the degree in which they are affected. Obviously, this raises a crucial problem about what interests are to be accounted legitimate. Interpreted conservatively it could mean that all existing interests are to be protected. Interpreted radically, it might seem that everything is 'up for grabs' and every individual or group has an interest in almost everything. I shall attempt to show how a course might be steered between these extremes.

The first element of my strategy, then, is not only anti-state but anti-communalist, directed against giving sovereignty or anything like it to *any* geographically or ethnically circumscribed group. In doing so it runs contrary both to the major tradition of political philosophy and the course of political history, as well as to most projections for the future, conservative or radical. Nevertheless, I shall argue that the problems we have to face in practice can be solved only by moving in the direction of functional decentralization of this kind. My argument will involve an examination of the inherent characteristic of the various decision-making procedures that already exist in social practice designed to demonstrate their limitations and the effects of using them beyond the scope of those limitations. In particular, I shall examine the limitations of the market, bureaucracy and voting as mechanisms for the control of productive resources and argue that other mechanisms could be introduced that would not have the same limitations.

If the division of communal and corporate agencies into specialized functional agencies were carried as far as possible, subject to considerations of technical efficiency, the number of decision-making bodies with considerable autonomy would be increased enormously. Even at a municipal level there is no reason why the various services that local councils provide, roads, parks, libraries, recreation facilities, building regulations, health services, garbage collection and so on, should not be run quite independently of each other, with different geographical circumscriptions and with closer relations to similar services in other areas than to many other services in their own area. People might come to see themselves as being part of many diverse social activities and functional communities rather than any simple inclusive community. Indeed, this is increasingly the case in modern urban societies. Nevertheless the very complexity of modern life raises a seemingly intractable practical difficulty. In most local communities there is little enough interest in local politics. If people are faced with the need to participate actively in the very large range of agencies of all shapes and sizes that affect their well-being, it seems most unrealistic to suppose that they can or will do so in an informed and constructive way. In practice they will vote *en bloc* for party tickets and hand over their active voice to political elites.

III STATISTICAL REPRESENTATION

This brings me to the second and more outrageous element of my strategy. In order to have democracy we must abandon elections, and in most cases referendums, and revert to the ancient principle of choosing by lot those who are to hold various public offices.[2] Decision-making bodies should be statistically representative of those affected by their decisions. The illusory control exercised by voting for representatives has to be replaced by the chance of nominating and being selected as an active participant in the formulation of decisions. Elections, I shall argue, inherently breed oligarchies. Democracy is possible only if the decision-makers are *a representative sample* of the people concerned. I shall call a polity based on this principle a demarchy,[3] using 'democracy' to cover both electoral democracy and demarchy. How and under what conditions this procedure might work I shall discuss in detail later. For the moment I shall say just a little about the philosophical consequences of adopting it.

Until about two hundred years ago it was widely assumed that the principle of rotation of offices by lot was the characteristic procedure of democracy.[4] Since then democracy has come to be identified with competitive elections on an universal suffrage. In practice, this situation has arisen because democratization has usually been won by a series of steps, each of which has been mainly a matter of bringing existing political elites under the control of a wider group of the population by submitting them to the necessity of competing for office at regular intervals. It has rarely been a major tendency of such changes to widen the political elites themselves. When new groups have acquired the franchise they have often sought to generate their own political parties, but the elites that constitute the ruling stratum in these parties have usually come to be only superficially distinguishable from the more traditional elites. Elitism has not been challenged effectively.

In the theory of democracy two quite different strands of classical liberal theory have contributed to the identification of democracy with elections. Classical utilitarianism claims that actions are to be evaluated solely by their consequences. What matters is that governmental decisions should be good decisions. The responsibility of decision-makers is not to give people what they want, but what is in their interest. The role of elections is to give electors the chance of choosing those who are best equipped to make good decisions, those who possess all the knowledge and skill that the electors themselves inevitably lack. By contrast, a less clearly formulated tradition, often associated with Rousseau and more generally with contractual views of political authority, sees elections essentially as the expression of the collective will of the electors. The government derives its legitimacy not from its function or its deeds and their consequences but from a commission given to it by an agreed procedure of electoral choice. A governmental agency ought to do all and only those things that the majority of the electors want it to do.

The utilitarian position about elections depends primarily on factual considerations. Elections are supposed to be the best means we have of seeing that government is properly carried on. So my differences with them will be resolved by the discussion of the possibility and consequences of statistically representative democracy or demarchy. (I am not a utilitarian but the differences do not matter in this context.) The contractual tradition, however, raises more complex questions. One might argue, for example, that a voluntarist account of political authority is compatible with any form of government, since the people can will anything that they like. But the voluntarist view may be pressed so far that only those particular decisions that command informed, universal and explicit consent are deemed legitimate. In that case any substantial existing interest group is in a position to block any change that affects its interests adversely. Even if the requirement of consent is restricted to decision procedures rather than extended to specific decisions, no group would consent freely and rationally to decision procedures that would undermine its vital interests.[5] Some contractarians, notably John Rawls, have held that it is possible to escape the problems of actual interests and to deduce a set of moral principles of legitimacy from a thought experiment. This envisages a group of people who are ignorant of what their interests will be convening to decide on a constitution that will be beneficial to the contractants no matter what their interests may turn out to be.[6] These moral principles would then act as constraints on what could be deemed a legitimate will. I believe that such hopes of deriving definitive results from thought experiments are theoretically and practically illusory. Nevertheless, given some fairly weak assumptions, I believe that the Rawlsian move constitutes a reasonable test that any proposal calling itself democratic should pass. I believe that my proposal would pass.

At the other end of the scale from extreme individualist voluntarist views we come to views that attribute to the corporate will of the people a more or less mystical rightness. This will is not the product of compromises between conflicting interests or of accepted constitutional procedures but of historical necessity or of some *Volksgeist*. In so far as it attains concrete expression it is manifested in a charismatic leader or an organization that claims some unique authority to articulate it correctly. It is hardly necessary to emphasize either the enormous dangers of such movements or the ease with which they may in fact constitute a very effective social force in certain circumstances. One of the salient features of the sort of polity I am advocating is that it radically undercuts the possibility of such movements using the instruments of government to force their will on people. Indeed, I should hope that it would result in the dissolution of the social basis of charismatic authority and destroy its grip on people. Even if it is true that many of us have some profound psychological need for identification of a non-rational kind with some totality that transcends us, perhaps we can satisfy this need by identifying with football teams rather than governments, 'historic missions' or the destinies of races.

Nevertheless, no profound social change can take place in a conscious and deliberately controlled way unless there is a very wide consensus that it is at least acceptable, and a substantial group that is both strongly motivated and organized to bring it about. I concede that the central requirement in our present historical situation is that the working class should become conscious of the need to abolish the sources of class division at every level of social life. This is especially the case in the matter of control of the means of production. To that extent I agree with the classical Marxist analysis. What that analysis lacked in my view, however, was a sufficiently rigorous theory of democratic government.[7] Rather, the classical Marxists tended to share the anarchist assumption that in the struggle for democracy the revolutionary movement would generate spontaneously the decision procedures and institutions that were needed to produce a democratic society. I shall argue that in this respect it was deeply mistaken and try to indicate the strategies that are appropriate for a revolutionary socio-political change in a democratic direction.

IV ASSUMPTIONS

Demarchy, as I shall present it, is utopian, at least in the sense that no model for it exists, and it is not based on a projection of present trends or causes. It can be brought about, if at all, only by convincing enough people that it should be tried. Obviously the chances of doing that are small. So it is all the more important to emphasize that in other respects it is not utopian at all. In particular, I shall argue that it does not presuppose that people perform substantially better either morally or intellectually than they do at present. My hope is that it could create conditions that would lead to improvements in the level of moral and scientific self-awareness in the community through a self-reinforcing process, but there are good grounds for embracing it without putting any store by such hopes. It is offered primarily as a solution to present problems, a way of averting very great evils, starting with small practical steps.

Meanwhile, the lack of any clear and plausible view of how a democratic socialist society might work is, I believe, the main obstacle to significant radical activity. State socialism in all its forms has been discredited. It has become increasingly difficult to put all the failures down to exogenous causes. The kinds of changes that *can* be produced by the use of centralized power are not the changes most socialists had hoped for. Moreover, popular spontaneous action is clearly no remedy. At best it is haphazard, ill-coordinated, often foolish and short-lived. At worst, it is terror manipulated by leaders engaged in power struggles. The fond hopes of the anarchists, which Marx himself and so many Marxists have shared, that the solutions to how future society is to be governed will emerge in the process of struggle have proved illusory. Organized struggle to control the state calls for military and political organization of a centralized and authoritarian kind. It reproduces state power transferring it into the hands of different people. Unorganized struggle merely forces the existing power structure to adapt. It cannot replace that structure.

Still it will appear absurd to many to offer a few changes in procedure as a solution to the great problems of our time. It smacks of panaceas and monomanias, like Berkeley's faith in tar water. Blanket scepticism, however, is no more rational than credulity. Procedures are very important, especially where it is a question of producing decisions from a mass of disparate inputs that can be interrelated in a variety of ways. In order to produce reliably good quality output a sound procedure is needed both to select good quality input and to process it properly. In social decision-making the crucial questions are, What kinds of information about the situation can the decision process handle? What desires and aspirations does it respond to? How good is it at coming up with the most practical and appropriate decisions in the circumstances?

Decisions are made by people. Good people may arrive at good decisions in spite of poor institutionalized procedures, when they are not wholly constrained by those procedures. Conversely, the best procedures in the world can be misused by people who are determined to do so. But the more complex the society and the longer our time-span the less likely it is that these divergences from the norm will be significant. This is not just a matter of probabilities sorting themselves out in the long term. Procedures have a constraining effect on what is registered and what is made of it, and the constraints tend to grow tighter the more deeply entrenched the procedures become. If the success of a business enterprise is entirely a matter of its relative profitability, then it becomes increasingly difficult for a manager under the pressure of competition to take account of factors that produce no profit, even if there are other good reasons for doing so and the cost is not great. The manager becomes typecast in the role of profit producer. There may even be a suggestion of impropriety, at least in the eyes of accountants and shareholders, in stepping out of that role. It is not the manager's money that is involved. Similarly, judges are increasingly held to the letter of the law, bureaucrats to regulations and politicians to what generates the most favourable balance of power, whatever their personal preferences.

The crucial problem is that our present procedures of public decision-making are incapable of registering reliably a number of aspects of the situation that are of great concern to those who understand them, and incapable of drawing reliably the appropriate conclusions even from the information they do register. Because they deal with vital questions they must be changed. The change will not be an improvement unless certain other conditions are present. Above all, there must be enough people who in their own interests are willing and able to make the changed procedures work. I shall argue that it is not unrealistic to suppose that there are enough such people, and that there are practical strategies of change available.

Similarly, I shall have to argue that it would be rational for people to accept the decision procedures I am advocating. My argument will be that it is much less risky to hand over control of public goods to a variety of very limited agencies than to one omnicompetent agency. The risk of irresponsible action is dispersed. Total disaster is less likely. However, the problem of control becomes more complicated. It is, superficially at least, much easier to keep a watch over a single authority than over very many. But the watch one can keep over an omnicompetent authority cannot be very effective. In any case, on most things that affect me I have no particular view, certainly no well-founded basis of assessment. I should be reasonably content to have those matters looked after by people who are competent, sensitive to my interests and are watched by others who share my needs. At the same time, I should like to have the opportunity of playing a substantive role in those few areas in which I have some stronger interest and knowledge, provided the benefits of doing so outweigh the costs.

By contrast with existing democratic practice, demarchy does not assume that most of the population is in a position to make soundly based assessments of all the major issues of government policy or even to assess the merits of rival elites competing for votes. What it assumes is that most people, if they are faced with limited concrete questions about matters that affect them directly, are capable of gaining enough understanding of the issues to make sensible choices about them. Moreover, it is not too difficult to arrange things so that they have sufficient inducements to act responsibly in these matters, to seek the best advice, open up discussion of the possibilities and attempt to find optimal solutions. Where more difficult, higher-level functions are involved, it is more likely that people with suitable competence and motivation can be found and chosen by and among those who have worked together on more limited problems than by any other selection process.

My pessimism about our present political structures is accompanied by a similar pessimism about our economic structures. I shall have to show how these too can be changed for the better. Again I shall argue that, granted reasonably realistic conditions, the crucial factor is the practices that constitute decision procedures in these matters. I make no pretensions to solve the problems of economic theory, nor do I draw very much on the many extensions of economic theory to matters of public choice. All of this work achieves a certain rigour at the cost of working with very limited and abstract models. These models can be applied to real situations only with a good deal of caution, which is often missing in their advocates.

By contrast, the considerations I shall offer are of a looser, but more practical kind, suggestive and exploratory rather than theoretical and explanatory. Ultimately, the only solid ground for asserting that something is possible is that it exists. Conceptual analysis can show that a state of affairs is conceivable, but it cannot pretend to show that the conception encompasses everything that is needed for it to be realized. So it cannot even assure us that a state of affairs is not impossible, much less that it is possible in some stronger sense, for example possible under certain given conditions. The strength of conceptual analysis lies in bringing out the contradictory characteristics of conceptions that at first sight appear quite reasonable. So I make no sweeping claims about the arguments offered in this book. They are designed to induce readers to give practical consideration to certain possibilities in the light of their own needs and experience. My justification for asking people to read this book is that if what I have to say is right it is very important, and it has not been said before. It is intended to provoke and challenge readers of every sort to say where it is wrong.

V THE ARGUMENT

Chapter 1 confronts the usual arguments for the necessity of the state in an attempt to undermine them, and underlines the dangers in the state system and the precariousness of attempts to control it. It is argued that the system of states generates rigidities and absurdities that are impossible to control democratically. In chapter 2 the problem of bureaucracy, control from the top through large permanent administrative organizations, is examined and the reasons for it criticized. The possibility of organizations being answerable directly to those affected by their decisions is explored and the problems of such a system clarified.

Chapter 3 undertakes a sustained critique of voting, emphasizing the paucity of the information a vote can convey, the futility of the individual vote in mass assemblies and the impossibility of voters becoming well informed. The defects of party politics and the incapacity of reforms in systems of voting to remedy them are detailed. This critique is followed by an argument that statistically representative decision-making bodies would provide a means of meeting all the major objections to electoral politics, as well as providing a means of breaking bureaucracies down into small units under the direct control of those they affect.

Chapter 4, having briefly surveyed the inadequacy of a pure market economy to provide public goods and reasonable access for all to the means of production, outlines a proposal for a market society in which various productive resources are vested in different trustee bodies. These trustees would be independent of each other and not subject to any central policy-making or executive body. They would lease productive resources to firms at prices that would cover the need for public goods, and safeguard other community requirements. The argument is that demarchy would constitute an adequate social control of production in a market economy and provide satisfactory security for all.

In chapter 5 various features of and objections to this system of public decision-making that I call 'demarchy' are examined, and the hopes that might reasonably be placed in it are detailed.

A reader who is anxious to get to the heart of the matter might start at chapter 3, or even at the third section of that chapter, where the working principles of demarchy are outlined, and proceed to chapters 4 and 5.

I have many ideas about the practical details of implementing demarchic principles that are not mentioned in this book. To do so would have been misleading. What I am anxious to produce is a radical reappraisal of the whole problem of public decision-making. Once people accept the possibility of demarchy they rapidly find themselves coming up with an abundance of suggestions about how it might work in practice. It is one of its great strengths that it makes experimentation in thought and practice infinitely easier than in state-governed societies. It thrives on diversity.

1
Democracy and the state

I THE STATE IS UNNECESSARY

Must there be some single organization in a given territory
that has a monopoly of legitimate force to deal with issues of
common interest and assert the common interest over all
more particular interests? Anarchists apart, all political
thinkers in modern times have thought so. Marxists have seen
the necessity of the state as historically provisional. Under
socialism it will wither away. Other historically minded
theorists have stressed that abstract conceptions of the state
neglect the radical differences between political organizations
in different epochs and circumstances. But most agree that
there are sound arguments that show that in any large society
a supreme authority is indispensable for the foreseeable
future.

   In spite of all efforts to sanctify or justify it the state remains
a paradox, the great Leviathan that is meant to suppress
violence by monopolizing it, the supreme constraint on our
liberties that is meant to guarantee liberty, the provider of
goods with an inexhaustible appetite for taxation. In its central function as the monopolist in the provision of peace and
order the state is quite literally a protection racket. It insists
that we buy its protection whether we want it or not. If we try
to deal with another firm we are punished as rebels or
traitors. Moreover, the need for the sort of protection the
state supplies takes the particular form that it does as a direct

result of the system of states. It is because of the concentrations of power that states make possible that nothing less
than the power of a state can protect us. We are so afraid of
what states can do to people that we must have our own. Of
course states provide many other public services besides
defence and policing, and many of these are less spurious.
But that it has fallen to the state to provide them is due
almost wholly to the fact that the state has a monopoly on
legitimate violence. There are alternatives. There can be
legitimate authorities quite independently of the state, and it
is possible for them to have adequate sanctions to ensure that
they are obeyed.

Community

Even many anarchists agree that the only alternative to the
state is community control,[1] which is only possible in groups
small enough for their members to share many common
beliefs, and to have direct and many-sided relations among
themselves, including many involving reciprocity, particularly mutual assistance but also retaliation. All societies need
to enforce a variety of actions and abstentions from action.
They must be able to do this by social pressure if they are to
escape the need for a police force and a state. In a large
anonymous community it is too easy to evade social pressure.

The argument is by no means decisive. I shall argue that the
crucial problem is that of controlling not individuals but
organizations. A multiplicity of authorities with specialized
competences and activities could be co-ordinated without being subordinate to any single overarching authority. Basically
they would co-ordinate their activities by negotiation among
themselves. Of course such specialized authorities could come
into conflict between themselves and there would need to be
some body with authority to settle their differences authori-
tatively. But it is at least conceivable that such a body might
have only an arbitrating function, with no right to dictate

policy. Its only sanction might be that most individuals and organizations would accept its verdicts and enforce them against recalcitrants by peaceable means, boycotts, disobedience and moral pressures. Such a state of affairs would presuppose that the society did not generate organizations with interests that were so wide ranging, self-contained and strong as to enable them to defy community sanctions. I shall argue that specialization of function could ensure that no large body of people had so strong an identification with any one organization as to regard it as representing uniquely their supreme interests. People would see themselves as belonging to a large number of overlapping communities, not to any single total community at any level. It will be part of my task to show how such a decentralization of power might be possible in societies of a very high degree of complexity.

In effect I shall argue that specialized organizations can themselves form communities of organizations, highly analogous to communities of individuals. Just as mutual interaction and interdependence against the background of shared beliefs and practices can produce a stable order among individuals and families, the same factors can discipline organizations, under certain conditions. Among those conditions are that no organization is self-sufficient, none is in a position to dictate to the others, and that each organization has a strong incentive to co-operate with others even where there is no immediate pay-off in doing so. Satisfying these conditions presupposes that there are effective barriers to individuals and groups getting control of enough organizations to subvert the patterns of mutual interdependence and turn them into largely one-way relations of power. I shall show how this is possible. Meanwhile let us take stock of the other arguments for the necessity of the state.

Violence

The first of these arguments is essentially Hobbesian. There is a tendency among human beings to settle their arguments by violence. The tendency for the use of violence to lead to further violence in a self-reinforcing process can be halted only by an authority powerful enough to suppress the use of violence by all others. The argument applies not only to individuals but to organizations, and so to states themselves. It need not rest on any claim that we have an innate disposition to violence. It is sufficient that from time to time we do use it, and that violence breeds violence. Ultimately world peace demands a world state, a supreme monopoly of effective legitimate violence.

In order to answer this argument we need to distinguish three main areas in which violence must be controlled. The first is that of violent crime, where individuals or small groups use violence for gain or personal satisfaction against other individuals and groups whose recognized rights they violate. This, I shall argue, can be handled in well-established ways, and the agencies needed for controlling it can themselves be controlled by demarchic institutions, especially if these agencies are relatively specialized or local. There will always be problems in this area, though some of the worst of them would be reduced if societies did not persist in attempting to control so much of people's behaviour.

The second area is that of the use of violence for political ends against an established order. This kind of violence is rare and relatively easily controlled where the order is commonly accepted and just and its normal institutions function well. It should not be a problem in a demarchy, particularly because there would be no powerful state apparatus that the insurgents could hope to control or subvert.

The third is that of states themselves, or of groups acting with a state's connivance, where there is no commonly recognized and enforced basis of justice between the contending parties. In 'state of nature' situations of the kind envisaged by Hobbes even very small groups may be involved in violent conflict of this sort, and it may even be that the state was an historical necessity for humankind to get beyond cer-

tain historical situations. In its more primitive forms, however, radical conflict depended for its attractiveness not only
on the absence of a law-enforcing state, but also on the
simplicity of the productive relations and technology of
hunter-gatherer and largely agricultural societies. One could
simply kill, expel or enslave the conquered population and
immediately set up in production on their territory. Under
modern conditions effective conquest is a very much more
complex and difficult business to carry through effectively
and profitably. Keeping large subject populations in order is
an expensive and not particularly cost-effective enterprise.
Only the resources and organization of the state make it
possible. Only 'reasons of state', and state aggrandizement
and paranoia, make it attractive. Economically it is almost
always cheaper to buy coal than to 'mine it with bayonets'.
The key to extirpating state violence is the abolition of the
state as we know it.

There is no way of abolishing particular states without
abolishing the system of states. As long as one national community confronts others that are organized as nation-states, it
too must take the form of a nation-state. In particular, it
must be prepared for war. There is at the present time no adequate guarantee of the security of any nation-state that is
not prepared to defend itself by force. It has often been
argued that, short of a world state, there cannot be. But that
is false. What is required is not some higher body more
powerful than any of its subordinates but the removal of
causes of war and disarmament. Short of that, a nation with
a well-entrenched pattern of decentralized government might
well be able to make the cost to a foreign power of attempting
to take it over too high to be worth the effort. In the absence
of any centralized chain of command there would be no point
in attempting to use the existing machinery of government.
An aggressor might, of course, succeed in taking control of
some key facilities that were particularly significant to it but it
is unlikely that it could secure the sort of co-operation in their

own suppression that conquered states commonly extend to their conquerors.

At the same time other functions of states could be internationalized. There already are some international agencies that exercise considerable authority in specific areas.[2] If we restrict ourselves to questions of abstract possibility there is little doubt that many functions of nation states could be transferred to such bodies, to the advantage of practically everybody affected. There is no compelling reason why all the functions of the nation state should not be dispersed to more limited agencies from the point of view of functional necessities, or even advantages.

Obviously, in practice the difficulties are insurmountable in the present state of the world. There is no adequate common political culture that could provide the basis for the authority of such bodies, except perhaps in those areas where such bodies as the international scientific community would be the main relevant constituency. The tendency of nation states is to stress and promote ideological differences between national groups. Even more importantly, the vast disparities of economic power between nations, the trap of underdevelopment and exploitation, have largely destroyed Marx's vision of a genuinely and effectively international movement of the economically oppressed. Even where they do not actively support national chauvinism or imperialism, workers in advanced countries are desperately afraid of the effect of immigration and competition from their poorer counterparts in underdeveloped countries. They are determined not to abrogate any of the collective goods that the relatively high wealth of their communities guarantees to them. On the other hand, the poor nations fear that international agencies would work in favour of the rich and cling desperately to their mostly illusory political independence.

Nevertheless, if we are to take the measure of the problems that face human beings in general and the oppressed in particular, it is vital that we do not deny the existence of problems simply because they are at present intractable. At the worst it may be that only a global catastrophe, most probably a full-scale nuclear war, could change the situation and people's perceptions of it so as to make a radical movement towards the abolition of states possible. At best, there might be a series of fairly specific crises that would lead to the formation of more international authorities leading up to the crucial step of disarmament and the gradual abandonment of the traditional conception of sovereignty. In either case progress is unlikely to be made unless there is a widespread conviction that the only satisfactory solutions are those that constitute advances towards whittling away the state.

It has not always been obvious to everybody that the recourse to violence to settle disputes is a bad thing. Willingness to risk one's life to affirm what one believes in has often been seen as the supreme test for 'manhood', or even of spiritual worth. Wars have been seen as the indispensable solvents of rigid and anachronistic forms of life, the means of social change. They have been compared to the great storms that, as the metaphor would have it, purify the seas and lakes by destroying the polluted stagnation of peace. Only in ultimate conflict, it is alleged, can a whole people rise above its petty particular interests and assert a common and transcendent interest that is both nobler and more truly rational than any lesser good.

Such arguments are utterly specious. Wars are always waged for particular, and usually illusory, interests. It is a much greater and more difficult thing to work consistently and constructively for a common good than to risk one's life for it. There is nothing inherently noble about risking death. People risk their lives every day for transient thrills. The element of truth in this romantic view of war is that one ought not to allow oneself to be coerced by the threat of force into abandoning something worth defending. But it is infinitely more desirable to find ways in which the threat of force can be eliminated. There may indeed be good reasons for using violence to overthrow oppressive regimes. But that necessity arises from the monopoly of power enjoyed by particular groups, not from the desirability of violence as such. The danger of rigidity and stagnation is a function of entrenched power, not of peace. There is no reason to believe that a decentralized society would not be one of rapid and healthy non-violent change.

Integration of the common good

The second argument for the necessity of the state questions this last assertion. It sees the common good as an integrated whole that can be achieved only by concerted and authoritative action planned and sanctioned by a very powerful central authority. This view is usually associated with 'communism' or state socialism, but it clearly has conservative proponents as well. It emphasizes not so much the danger of particularist violence, as traditional liberals did, but the constructive task of building a genuinely common good. That good not only comprises an integrated set of material conditions in which individuals and groups can flourish but encourages and enforces specific social relationships and a subordination of the individual to the common good. This argument is not incompatible with many versions of the argument regarding violence but insists that violence is only a secondary aspect of the problem.

All that can come out of a decentralized polity, it insists, is a series of limited, *ad hoc* compromises between existing interests that leave the broader and deeper problems of social structure and relationships untouched. The historic roles of nations or classes cannot be reduced to piecemeal changes. The will of the people cannot be reduced to some simple function of particular interests or wills. It must be articulated and expressed in common action, leadership and organization, through which people can recognize and respond to a vision and a reality that eludes more myopic views.[3]

It is possible, and, I believe, correct, to concede a good deal of force to the premises of this argument. The common good is in many of its components something that can only be possessed collectively. It is like a game in which an individual participates but cannot play on her own. But common goods in this sense can exist without there being a single authority that is charged with producing them. Even where some specific common good needs an authority to organize it, or a variety of common goods must be co-ordinated, there is no compelling reason for such a task to fall to a state. Many of our most important cultural goods, our languages, arts and sciences, have been produced without the state playing any substantial constructive role in their production. Decentralized societies do not have to be individualistic or lacking in communal organizations and recognized authorities.

What is at issue is not the production of common goods but control over that production. That democratic control over the production of common goods is seen in terms of democratic control of the state is simply a result of the role that the state has made for itself. The state dominates the units that we call 'peoples', forcing homogeneity on its population through educational, legal and economic policies, integrating diverse goods into a single package. So 'the people' come to be defined as the citizens of a nation state, and their interests as the totality of interests that the state can encompass. Granted this situation, realistic democrats recognize that a mass electorate can articulate an opinion only about the major direction of administration and legislation. So, if the people are to have a say through the electoral process on the major questions of government, they must exercise their power through a central authority that attempts to give specific expression to the will of the people through a host of co-ordinated decisions. The more control is centralized the more likely it is that a genuinely common interest transcending particular entrenched interests will prevail.

Some of the arguments against this view have become very familiar. A highly centralized administration can control a vast number of particular operations only through a bureaucracy that inserts many levels of decision-making between broad policy decisions at the top and final implementation at the bottom level. Bureaucracies tend to be rigid and have a high degree of inertia. They function on the basis of rules that are designed with more attention to ease of administration than to the substantive interests they are meant to serve. Diversity, experimentation, flexibility are sacrificed to uniformity, the avoidance of risk and predictability. The bureaucracy puts very tight limits on what its master can do. It controls the formulation of specific proposals. It controls the flow and form of information. It monopolizes expertise. The better it is at its tasks the more difficult it is to control, to change, to challenge.

These costs might be bearable if the bureaucracy did in fact achieve some desirable kind of rational co-ordination of public policy over a wide domain. But in fact the bureaucracies of various departments of government are often more concerned to prevent incursions of other departments into their domain than to co-operate with them. At the most particular level, a road being resurfaced seems to ensure that some other authority will dig it up next week to lay new cables or pipes. At the highest levels bureaucrats soon establish a symbiotic relationship with the particular interests they are supposed to control and devote themselves to the defence and advancement of those interests at the expense of conflicting interests.

No doubt a strong and determined government can bring a bureaucracy to heel, reorganize and redirect it. Revolution from above is possible at the cost of a great deal of authoritarian administration. But ultimately the effect of such methods is to transform the old bureaucracy into a new one that is vastly more powerful and rigid than its predecessor. Gentler and more gradualist uses of bureaucracy as a means of social transformation tend to produce precisely that piecemeal accommodation to particular interests that centralized power is supposed to avert. In a relatively free society it evokes a proliferation of organized interest groups that demand and get all sorts of concessions, subsidies and exceptions, often institutionalized in special agencies, that effectively nullify the sweep of general policy, especially where those groups have specific bases of economic, ideological or electoral power.

These counter-arguments to the centralization of power are, I believe, decisive if one sets a high value on democratically controlled social change. However, even the conservatives, valuing stability and continuity above innovation and experiment have reason to be disenchanted with bureaucracy. Its mechanical and instrumental rationality is hardly conducive to the flexibile, consensual ways of dealing with social problems that they wish to promote.[4] They do not know how such an ideal is to be given concrete form in a very complex and unstable society. So they have proved very vulnerable to the so-called neo-conservatives who preach a fundamentalist version of classical liberalism.

Dividing the cake

The more fundamental counter to the argument that strong central authority is necessary to produce a coherent common good is to question its basic premises and presuppositions.

The idea that an unified social policy is desirable can rest on a variety of bases. One is that there is some good that is of such over-riding importance that it must be promoted or protected above every other and that only a supremely powerful organization can do this. At times this may be the case, but the assumption that there is such a good and that the state can protect it, or is the only way of protecting it, must always be subject to intense scrutiny. The state usually devours what it is supposed to protect. A slightly weaker form of this view is that there is a firm list of priorities that must be imposed on recalcitrant institutions, groups and individuals, and that a supreme authority is necessary to do so. Against such assumptions I shall argue that there are ways of so governing specific functional institutions that they work directly for the common good without being subject to any higher government.

The common good is an interrelated set of more specific goods that are not to be identified simply as the goods of particular individuals or groups. Rather they are the good functioning of a variety of institutions, practices and resources that interest many different individuals and groups in a variety of ways and degrees. What is important for each of these instrumentalities in terms of social co-ordination is that the other related institutions, practices and resources that it does not control function in ways that provide favourable conditions for its own functioning. The best way of achieving this is by direct negotiation between various specialized authorities directed to producing arrangements that are mutually advantageous. Failing that, some form of arbitration between them should produce a more satisfactory solution than any persistent intervention from a higher level. If each of these bodies for producing some public good does its job *qua* producer of public goods in the light of the interests of those involved with that good, the result should be that the complex that is the common good will be better served than by any attempt to articulate it from above.

The crucial questions are, How can those who make the decisions in these specific agencies be in touch with the needs they are supposed to serve, and the relevant expertise about what is possible? How can they be encouraged adequately or, if need be, constrained to act in the interests of the public good? How can they be chosen and prevented from becoming entrenched? These are central questions that I believe I can answer. For the moment I ask that it be granted for the sake of argument that my answers are satisfactory. One crucial question remains, however, namely that of adjudicating between conflicting claims to scarce resources. Let us ignore for a moment the question, Where do the resources come from? Still, dividing up the resources involves a very important degree of policy decision and control. Are we not left with something suspiciously like a state? Who pays the piper calls the tune. The allocation of resources is, in the short run at least, a zero-sum game. That does not mean that it must be run by a single authority. There could be a variety of bodies that allocate finance to various institutions and projects, each making its grants conditional on the receipt or non-receipt of grants from other sources. Such a system might be quite flexible and efficient if the membership of various granting bodies were competent and reliable. It could, I shall argue, even be democratic if the granting bodies were representative of the whole spectrum of interests in the community.[5]

Law

Even if it is the case that there is no compelling reason for material public goods to be produced or supervised by a central authority, the common good includes at least one vital element that appears necessarily to involve a central authority, namely law. Decentralized powers must be defined and machinery of arbitration set up. Bodies such as those we have been suggesting can only be stable and legitimate if constituted and supported by law. In very complex and artificial societies there are no 'natural' authorities of the sort that there may be in simple or traditional societies. The scope, functions, entitlements and limits of specific authorities need constantly to be redefined in the light of changed circumstances. The scope and limits of entitlements, rights and duties must be spelled out so that people can know what they can and cannot do. The law must not only articulate what is valid or invalid, it must punish wrongs and protect those who are not able to protect themselves. Above all it must express a common conception of justice and seek to promote it.

Some kinds of dispute may be settled by recognized arbitrators without any explicit legislative or juridical system, but clearly many could not in any complex society. This is a point that I do not propose to deny. What I do deny is that it entails the sort of power that is given to modern states. There might be a plurality of law-making bodies for specific functional rather than geographical areas, a sort of federalism of function. In such a polity the role of any supreme legislature and supreme court might be quite limited, consisting for the most part of reviews of and appeals from laws and decisions of more specialized authorities, and readjustments to their jurisdictions and procedures, without any power to initiate judgement on substantive 'first order' questions. Such executive functions as were necessary to carry out legal decisions might be exercised directly by the courts without any independent executive arm being necessary. Such an authority would rely on invoking community sanctions against recalcitrant authorities rather than exercising specific penal powers such as fines or imprisonment. It would rest its authority on the common recognition of its right to make these decisions and the importance and general acceptability of the decisions themselves.

No doubt a widely shared democratic political culture would be an indispensable condition of the operation of an institution such as I have sketched. Institutions and practices do not function automatically and without preconditions. Even in present states the effect of such a culture on the functioning of political institutions is not achieved primarily by force or the sanctions of electoral success and failure. It is to a very great extent a matter of what people are prepared to accept as right or at least reasonable. Even those who do not accept the substance of that culture are forced to give at least an hypocritical endorsement to its externals. I assume that the present aspirations for rational, just and responsive decision-making in public affairs are capable of substantial development and that increasing the variety and specificity of the institutions in which public affairs are conducted would produce greater participation in and awareness of a shared political culture and in turn enrich that culture. I shall try to show in detail how this might be brought about.

II WHY WE SHOULD GET RID OF THE STATE

In the preceding paragraphs I have been assuming that it is desirable to get rid of the state for two obvious reasons. The state is the means of war and of repression. Whether one adopts the view that human beings are naturally territorial and bellicose or naturally peaceable and reasonable the conclusion is the same. If they are bellicose it is folly to let modern weapons of destruction fall into their hands. If they are peaceable there is no good reason for running the risk of mistakes and accidents. In any case whatever innate dispositions people, or significant proportions of them, may have, these are heavily overlaid by training, repression and social organization. No matter how one attempts to romanticize violence, it is supreme folly to put ourselves in the hands of the few who, at the touch of a button, can unleash incalculable and irreversible destruction upon humankind.

Even apart from war and the threat of war, the repressive potential of the state is enormous and largely uncontrollable. This potential may not be apparent where the society is not under great strain or overt conflict. The capacity to escape such strains, however, is much more the exceptional case than the norm.

I shall return to this point later when various other economic and social theses have been argued.

Functions of the state

Meanwhile, let us look more closely at the functions of the modern state. The state exists to express and promote the unity of a given territorial community. Its monopoly of legitimate violence has been used to attempt to safeguard and promote a great variety of things that have been regarded as important to the community: its military power relative to other states, its religious and other culturally important beliefs, its internal law and order, its economic well-being and its prestige. It has an ideological function, a military one and an economic one. The history of the modern state system is a history of struggles about the exercise of these functions, various forces striving to maximize or minimize each or all of them or to produce decisive shifts in policy in each or all of them.

The net effect of these struggles has been a vast increase in the scope and efficacy of state operations and a marked change in their characteristic forms and modes. Even those who have been hostile to the state and to the particular socioeconomic order that it buttresses have by and large succeeded only in extending the range or changing the mode of its operations. Some of the disabilities of the oppressed have been alleviated by social services of many kinds, at the cost of making the recipients clients of the state. Abuses have been controlled at the cost of proliferating agencies of state regulation. Greater economic stability has been achieved at the price of massive intervention by state agencies in the economy. In electoral regimes parties compete for votes by offering to use state power to the pretended advantage of various groups. Even the advocates of the minimal state succeed only in transferring the emphasis on welfare to an emphasis on armaments and 'law and order', strengthening one branch of the state at the expense of others and one segment of the community at the expense of others.

This enormously complicated organization is the site of a host of conflicts between fragmented interest groups. In Robert Dahl's phrase, what we have is not majority rule or minority rule but *minorities* rule, according to the ever-changing opportunities for diverse particular interests to gain some partial ascendancy over policy-making and its implementation in some specific areas. Within a limited perspective this sort of polyarchy, as Dahl aptly calls it, is on balance desirable. It mitigates the formal concentration of power and breaks down the tendency to bureaucratic inflexibility. Most groups get some relief from their most pressing problems. No group is in a decisive position on every issue. A certain sort of stability is achieved together with a significant degree of adaptability.

Such a view seems a far cry from Marx's view expressed in the aphorism that 'the executive of the modern state is the committee for handling the common affairs of the bourgeoisie'. Marx, of course, spoke only of the executive. He was aware that the state, even in his day, was much more than that. Contemporary Marxists have tried to cope with the problem of understanding the enormous qualitative and quantitative changes in the role of the state over the past hundred years or more.[6] At a very high level of generality it is easy enough to keep the substance of Marx's thesis intact. Modern states in the Western world, even when their governments profess some 'socialist' ideology, all maintain the capitalist system, and at least to that extent the central common interests of the bourgeoisie. Moreover in economic matters they are tightly constrained to safeguard the central motor of capitalism, the accumulation of capital, and their policies in other areas are closely governed by this central requirement.

In most countries the central electoral issues are issues of 'economic management'. Governments are made and unmade by perceptions of their success in administering the existing economic order. Attempts at even relatively modest change are rarely successful and produce great apprehension. The state is not a capitalist conspiracy, but it serves capital well. The commonly perceived alternative is state socialism and the evidence that that would be worse is generally regarded as overwhelming. Radical theorists may talk of various possibilities of socialism without the state, but there are no practical political programmes for achieving it, and its very possibility remains highly debatable. The capitalist state is generally accepted. It is no doubt a site of class struggle, but that struggle has rarely taken any radical orientation. It is not a struggle for a decisive socio-economic change but for small readjustments of policy that leave the system intact.

In the middle of the nineteenth century both conservatives and radicals thought that the advent of full adult suffrage would herald a decisive political class confrontation. The have-nots would dispossess the haves, the repressive apparatus of the state would be destroyed, and the dictatorship of the proletariat would inaugurate either a new tyranny or a new freedom in democracy. Five generations later these hopes and fears have been decisively disappointed. By and large the state is not perceived by the workers as the prime instrument of class oppression. For it is not, for the most part, overtly repressive.

The mode of state control has changed, as Foucault has emphasized, from overt show of force on sporadic occasions to a pervasive surveillance and regulation of vast areas of social life.[7] As long as one goes about one's ordinary occupations in the normal way one is hardly conscious of the state's omnipresent regulation. Very often it appears as a protective shield, a big brother much more benign and permissive than Orwell's fiction. In 1984 one cannot take *1984* very seriously most of the time, at least as it affects most people in most democratic countries. The purported demonstration that the state is deeply oppressive seems excessively metaphysical. Protest pays. Even the most entrenched bureaucrats want to appear fair and compassionate. The police are brutal and arbitrary only with those who are marginal to the community and deviant from its broad consensus. That consensus changes to incorporate and domesticate even more of the rebellious.

Strains in the system

Nevertheless, the state system is under very strong internal strains. In the first place, in advanced countries the state has to appropriate rarely less than a third and sometimes more than half of the gross national product to meet its commitments. Taxation is inherently arbitrary in its incidence. Even those who accept a given scheme of taxation almost always feel entitled to avoid its imposts. When large sums are involved evasion becomes an industry and every economic and political activity is affected by it. It stifles, corrupts and constrains what people can do. Even where taxation is formally redistributive from rich to poor it normally ends up being redistributive in the other direction, if only because the rich have so many more ways of evasion open to them and can afford the best advice on how to use them. The self-employed gain at the expense of the wage and salary earner, the unproductive speculator at the expense of the regular producer. Conversely, those who receive benefits from the state are placed under strong temptations to fake the bases of entitlement. Both tendencies can be countered only by even more detailed regulation and surveillance. Is there no better way of providing for public goods and for those in need of assistance?

In the second place, there is an insidious tyranny of numbers. The state homogenizes and atomizes social relationships. The horizons and expectations of people contract to the limits of those variations that the system constitutes as practical possibilities. Even where people are vaguely aware that things could be otherwise they often cling to the devil they know and find virtue in doing so. They settle for quiet passivity, shunning risk, experiment, confrontation and uncertainty. As the neo-conservatives have emphasized, they lose their resilience and initiative. Lacking something significant and constructive to do in public life they shrink into a private life that is increasingly trivial and boring. At worst they take to drugs, crime, charlatan religions and cynicism. The political culture on which the system depends is profoundly threatened.

Thirdly, nation states under internal strains have always tended to seek to overcome these strains by uniting the nation to respond to some real or contrived external threat. Threats lead to counter-threats and eventually to war, as the Falkland–Malvinas episode so recently reminded us.

Short of war, 'security' systems consistently increase the role of military and police power in society. Almost everywhere the military establishment is closely integrated with those forces in society that seek to maintain existing stratification and privileges, restrict information and debate and weaken the power of popular organizations of all sorts, especially trade unions and radical political groups. Most countries live under some degree of threat that the response to any significant shift of power away from the existing establishment will be military intervention, often direct military dictatorship. In any unstable situation the military are vastly better organized and better equipped to take the initiative effectively than any insurgent group can hope to be. Conversely, the greater the likelihood of confrontation with the military, the more any realistic radical group is likely to see itself forced to organize itself on military lines. The result is that even if it attains power it is likely to be as authoritarian and ultimately as reactionary in many respects as its opponents.

Fourthly, the military in most countries depend to some very significant degree on one or other of the superpowers for 'aid' in hardware, training and other support. They become pawns in the cold war, guardians of various forms of neo-colonialism. Poor nations devote scarce resources to armaments and economically and socially destructive organizations. Rich nations devote the little aid they are prepared to give to the poor mostly to military or para-military projects.

No doubt in a more fundamental analysis of the role of the state, the military would appear as secondary to basic economic and ideological forces. Nevertheless those forces could not operate or maintain themselves without the military and the state apparatus which in a crisis is always prepared to submit to military directions. The practical salience of military power is all but complete. A democratic state is a dialectical contradiction. The more powerful the state the less are people able to control it. The weaker the state the more power non-state elites enjoy. A state may, of course, in certain respects and under certain conditions, be more or less democratic, but only in conflict with its own inherent tendencies. The democratic state is an exceptional and unstable compromise. It is time to explore more deeply why this must be so.

III DEMOCRACY VERSUS THE STATE

In the liberal tradition there has always been a tension between a specific democratic ideal, the rule of the majority, and the view that the role of the state should be minimized in the interests of individual freedom. The freedom that was uppermost in the minds of the classical Anglo-American liberals was the freedom of the property-owning classes to dispose of their property as they saw fit. They feared that an envious propertyless majority would use their power to dispossess the rich and so ruin all classes. But there were other aspects as well.[8] Freedom of thought and expression, freedom of religion and freedom of association and movement were also important. A populist majority might be as intolerant as any absolute monarch.

The constitutional state

Their perceived solution to the problem was the constitutional state which had only those limited powers assigned to it in the constitution, or was expressly forbidden by the constitution from using its powers in certain specific ways. The guarantee of the constitution was the separation of powers, designed in such a way that each of the major functions of government kept a check on the others. Let us leave aside for the moment

the inadequacies and dangers of this system and concentrate
on the conception of democracy that came to be associated
with it. The dominant theme was that a democratic government was a minimal government. The liberal property-owner's
state could correspond to the interests of the overwhelming
majority of the people precisely because the people wanted to
be governed as little as possible. Their greatest interest was to
maximize their freedom. This in turn presupposed a society in
which the provision of goods by the state was unnecessary
because people were in a position to provide for themselves,
apart from the basic goods of law, defence and a minimal
infrastructure of facilities such as lighthouses. People would
see any unnecessary increase in state power as a threat to their
freedom. The will of the people was not to rule for fear of being ruled. An inherent contradiction between the state and
democracy was tacitly acknowledged, but in the limited and
unsatisfactory form.

The transition from the classical liberal to the liberal
democratic state rested on a change in its view of who constituted the people. As C. B. Macpherson has emphasized,
for the liberals it did not originally mean the whole population of the territory of the state, but rather the responsible
members of society, in practice owners of substantial property,
generally excluding not only women, slaves, foreigners and
criminals, but the vast majority whose only property was
their own labour power. Sometimes these, as servants, were
deemed to be represented by their masters. In any case they
were seen as lacking experience, education, good judgement
and a stake in the economic system. Not being free in their
daily occupations they were in no position to understand and
defend freedom.

It is easy to dismiss this conception of the people, as a self-
serving ideology promoted in the name of freedom by the
rising bourgeoisie, deriving its emotive force from its rejection of feudal privilege, but consecrating a new set of forms
of exploitation. In many respects, however, it was both more

honest and more realistic than the populist democracy to which it succumbed. It recognized that the state in fact functions to defend the existing social order, and that only those who have good reasons to support that order can be expected to make sound decisions about state policy. It aspired towards a rational administration of an actually functioning society rather than towards some illusory ideal. It realized clearly that the rule of the majority of inhabitants was not, at least in class societies, compatible with the stability of the state. Not just anything the majority may choose is politically possible. There can be a stable state only when there is basic harmony between the requirements of social and economic stability and the political power structure. Otherwise the state must either stand as a superior power above society and inevitably slide into tyranny or become the instrument of conflicting social forces. The normal result of the latter is a state of political chaos that also ends in tyranny.

Constricting the political agenda

The crucial way in which the system is safeguarded from fickle majorities is by narrowing the political agenda. If this has the happy result of preventing the state being used for some purposes in which its use is dangerous, it certainly does not prevent all such uses. More importantly for our present purpose, the fact that many urgent problems are distorted or not recognized as open to constructive solution is not just an effect of reactionary political tactics. It is endemic in the constitutional solution to the problem of tyranny. In the first place, the constitutional state remains a state. It cannot be an effective means of calling in question the consequences of the system of states. While nearly everybody would place the abolition of the arms race very high on their list of desiderata, the popular will for peace is almost wholly ineffectual. The state system cannot articulate such basic and pervasive needs realistically. It is nonsense to talk of rule by the people when such questions cannot even get on to the political agenda. Narrowly constricting the political agenda is an inevitable effect of constitutional government designed both to maintain and restrict the power of the state. One cannot exclude political tyranny without firmly entrenching institutions and practices that have a narrowly circumscribed scope and efficacy and a political culture that confines the tactics and issues of politics in the spirit of the constitution. It must become accepted that what is politically possible is limited and that it is right that these limits be observed.

The fact that constitutional politics cannot deal with those issues that bring into question the state system itself is not the only result. A host of other issues of vital importance are either effectively excluded from the horizon of practical politics or posed in a form that excludes awareness of appropriate solutions.

Fission suppressed

The most obvious rigidity is that states do not tolerate secession of any substantial part of their population. The very arbitrariness and precariousness of the boundaries of most states is the most powerful reason for their *not* being open to legitimate challenge. Once they are changed there is no particular natural limit to change. Conversely, states through a host of legal and 'educational' activities strive to suppress the cultural and economic bases of the distinct identity of lesser communities in an attempt to preserve the state's unity. The processes of free formation of communities are deliberately and effectively curtailed. The results are particularly damaging in places such as Africa where tribal and other community forms of development are still alive. As Michael Taylor emphasizes, fission has always been the normal means of evading internal conflict in communities. Deprived of this normal recourse communities that wish to resist absorption into the dominant state culture are repressed.

Paradoxically this repression is often hailed as a liberation. The old particular cultures are seen as outmoded and constricting, and their replacement by modern cultures is progress. Formally, of course, this is a liberation. The power of communities other than the state to exercise authority over their members is destroyed. It remains a very complex question whether freedom in one respect is not bought at the price of worse enslavement in another. Obviously many people affected by such changes feel that it is. The balance sheet for every community and every individual will be different. What is of more concern to us at present is whether or not non-state communities could tackle the sort of problems that arise when the material and technological bases of life are transformed to exploit modern scientific knowledge. The argument of this book is that they can, provided they are not total communities but overlap with a variety of other specialized communities in an open pattern.

If that is correct then the rigidity of the state system must be measured not only against all the destruction of minorities and their cultures for which it has been responsible but against the possibilities of a much more fluid and diverse political order that it excludes.

Collective property

The state is the supreme property-owner, enjoying the right of overriding all private property rights within its territory by resumption for public use, taxation, or punitive confiscation. It is only the law of the state that fixes determinate titles to property and what those titles entail in the enforceable exclusions of others. The state excludes itself from interfering with property only for reasons of prudence. One reason it cannot brook secession is that those seceding take with them part of its property.

Even more severely than any historical form of private property, state rights to property are sources of absolute exclusion of any responsibility to others. So the only ways in which other communities can obtain what they want from a state are by force, trade or appeals to pity. The poor communities remain poor because they lack resources with which to trade and force with which to threaten. The pity of the rich nations is miniscule.

If certain activities are to take place on a piece of land others must be excluded, at least temporarily. The farmer must exclude animals from grazing on the growing crop. But there can be a multiplicity of kinds of right to the exclusive use of land in particular ways under specific safeguards and for legitimate purposes. Various kinds of rights can belong to specific sorts of individuals and organizations. Assigning those rights need not rest on any overriding right, but simply on the authority to adjudicate conflicting claims.

What the state's supreme property rights express is an incoherent recognition that there is no natural claimant to the earth other than the whole community. Humankind, however, has no political existence. So each state acts in effect as if it were itself the whole, thus denying the rights of humankind as a whole. Once again it is easy to conclude that the problem can be solved only by the emergence of a world state that does represent all humankind. I am maintaining the contrary. Every all-embracing claim must be abolished and the system of entitlements changed to represent the real interest of the various overlapping communities that constitute the whole. Some of the *initial* moves in this reconstruction of property rights will involve the use of state power, but I hope to show how it need not depend on state power once it is launched.

Migration and population

One of the boasts of the liberal state is that, unlike most other states, it does not try to stop individuals and small groups leaving it. It does, however, impose severe restrictions on people joining it. Unquestionably, whom to exclude from group membership is one of the most difficult problems that any group has to solve. No group can absorb more members indefinitely without losing its original character, and having very different effects on its own members and on other groups. No group can fall below a certain size and still be viable. Nevertheless, where voluntary groups are concerned, we commonly uphold the freedom of people to leave them, much as we may regret the demise of the group. But joining is another matter. It is difficult to see precisely why this should be so. Clearly a group is entitled to set a fair price on the benefits that it provides for new entrants from the accumulated efforts of past members. Indeed, where the benefits are wholly the product of the members and impose no costs on others there is no compelling reason why the group may not exclude whom it likes and impose what price it likes on membership.

However, the most significant voluntary organizations do affect non-members' opportunities quite substantially. In some cases they have an effective monopoly of certain opportunities. A sporting club may for a variety of reasons have a monopoly on facilities for a particular sport in an area, a cultural club may have exclusive use of the facilities necessary for staging plays and concerts and so on. Where such monopolies exist it seems reasonable that clubs be required to admit appropriate applicants, at least up to the number at which it might reasonably be split into two viable clubs. But who is to lay down such requirements, on what authority and on what criteria?

There is a series of dilemmas that arise in any attempt to make such judgements. On the one hand, the group of voluntary associates ought to be able to determine their own way of doing things, the size of their membership and the rhythm of change in response to changing circumstances. Not only the liberty of the individuals but the diversity and spontaneity of social relations is at stake. From these points of view control is counterproductive. On the other hand, the strategic or monopoly power of voluntary organizations can be used to discriminate against people arbitrarily, and to enforce restrictive practices to the detriment not only of excluded individuals but of a range of social relationships. So we have various forms of anti-discrimination legislation. As we expand the scope and importance of the associations the problem becomes more acute.

In general, as I have suggested, and will argue more fully later, monopolies of material resources necessary for a particular activity should not be allowed to become a source of power for those who control or use them. The use of such resources should be subject to conditions that preserve the community interest. If one carries through that principle to the international situation then it seems that no nation should be permitted to have exclusive power over its own territory, but should enjoy it only subject to conditions that preserve the interests of other nations and their members. The nation itself should not have unqualified rights to exclude immigrants any more than to impose just any restrictions it likes on the sort of communities that are formed within its borders.

On the one hand, it is utterly unreasonable to expect any community or association or nation to maintain the sort of open door policy that can lead to its being destroyed in the way that the American Indian and Australian aboriginal communities were. Quite apart from the killing, plunder and treachery so conspicuous in those cases, the mere fact of overwhelming numbers of people, given to utterly new ways of social interaction, entering the territory in which a community lives can make it impossible to continue in the old ways or even to adapt constructively to the new circumstances. Communities of all sorts need time and elbow room if they are to preserve anything worthwhile through cultural and social change. It is not only in their interests but in the common interest that they be given the chance of dealing with external forces rather than being simply overwhelmed by them. On the other hand, the rigid demarcations that allow privilege to entrench itself are not in the long term interests of anybody or any community, at least once one discounts all claims to religious or cultural absolutes.

The state system, however, is just such a rigidly entrenched way of preventing free interchange of members between communities. The interests of a certain established community and power structure are preserved without regard to the needs of outsiders or the desirability of change within the nation.

Nations, states and community

A pure market system of relationships and a purely organizational system both put a premium on efficiency over other values. 'Instrumental rationality' is destructive of community. Flexible reciprocity, giving in the hope that one may get a similar service back from somebody else when one needs it, does not stand up in the context of strict contracts. Where each person looks after only his or her own interests and purposes, community norms and values wither. Where cash payments for specified tasks are the only basis of exchange the many-sided relationships that constitute communities wither. The nuclear family may succeed in insulating itself from these pressures because of the enormous internal pressures in favour of reciprocity that it generates. Small groups of families may extend some familial relations into areas of obvious mutual interest. Areas of civility may survive in more casual personal relationships, but community does not.

In these circumstances the crumbling identity of the nation finds expression only in the state and in a nostalgia that is wrongly called tradition. The nation not only attempts to use the state to assert its own reality and importance but strives to preserve itself by suppressing the very sources of internal variety and initiative that might give it life. The nation and non-formal communities more generally can maintain their identity through change only by adapting to meet the problems that threaten them. In general, in a complex world of increasingly specialized and differentiated activities no such open and flexible community can be a total community or be identified with a formal organization. It will destroy itself in the attempt, as so many nations have done.

At first sight the state represents the supreme example of reciprocity. It calls on its members to risk their lives for the nation, it preaches and (selectively) enforces a public morality of duty, service and altruism. But voluntary service is replaced by conscription, moral sanctions by law, and public service by professional careerism. The flexible, evolving common good of the nation is replaced by the goods that the state is designed to produce and regulate. Nationalism becoming statism ensures the death of those relationships that constituted the nation as a community and not just as an organization. The state, of course, has to keep alive the myth of the nation to justify its pretensions. People need to believe the myth because they have no other earthly hope of significant common achievement. But this myth is not the anticipation of an ideal. It is a mystification, a tragic illusion.

The need for an alternative

The most common complaint against contemporary liberal democracies is the remoteness of the decision-makers from those affected by decisions. Those affected have little say in those decisions unless they happen to be in a position to bring organized pressure on the decision-makers, and the ability to bring such pressure is very unequally distributed, usually in favour of groups that are already highly advantaged in their socio-economic power. But the present complaint is more fundamental. It concerns not only the existence of great inequalities in the distribution of power, but the incapacity of most people to do anything towards righting them. The result is a disillusionment with liberal politics among substantial groups in the community that threatens the political culture itself. A democracy that renders people impotent is no democracy.

It is not surprising, therefore, that realistic radicals have generally seen reformism as the enemy of any desirable attack on the problems generated by existing power relationships. If the people are to exercise power to change the system all constitutional limits on the exercise of power must be overthrown. But these very realists become utterly unrealistic when they are called on to answer how a popular or proletarian dictatorship is to be prevented from turning into the dictatorship of a small political elite. Even if we grant that the people can articulate what it finds objectionable in present practices and policies and the general direction in which they must be changed, it cannot articulate the concrete means by which changes are to be implemented. It is the particular things that are in fact done that have effects. The more these things are done through the exercise of state power by a small executive the more dangerous they are likely to be.

It is not just a question of the opportunity offered to the power hungry to pay lip-service to popular demands while entrenching repression, important though that is. It is not only that radical change must involve conflicts to which there is no right answer or that all specific conflicts become conflated with the basic conflict of 'the people' against its enemies. In practice the executive has to demand and enforce on the people the sort of discipline that a general must demand of an army once battle is joined. Since this demand itself creates new enemies the battle is never over, and the people have no more control over their leaders than privates have over generals.

The attempt to give more power to the people ends in tyranny over the people just as the attempt to exclude tyranny keeps the people from exercising power in the things that matter most. Neither the constitutional state nor the unlimited state can be controlled effectively by the people. Neither can do very much to improve the provision of public goods without increasing either the scope and rigidity of the state apparatus, or its arbitrariness and lack of accountability. Neither can be a means of calling into question the state system itself. Neither can offer satisfactory ways of dealing with the most pervasive social and economic problems. The question, Is democracy possible? is at least partially reducible to the question, Is it possible to provide for public and common needs by other institutions and practices than those of the state? If we are serious about answering this question it is not sufficient to point out the abstract possibility of alternatives to the state. We must give solid grounds for thinking that they could function effectively under realistic conditions.

2
Democracy and bureaucracy

I CAN WE DO WITHOUT BUREAUCRACY?

The case for bureaucracy

Bureaucracy is that form of permanent organization of social action that is directed by a central authority.[1] It is characteristic not only of state instrumentalities but also of large non-state institutions, business enterprises and universities, for example. Because the organization is permanent, most of its functioning elements are also permanent, and even the individuals who fill various offices in the organization are normally permanent and full-time members of it. Its various functions are regulated by fairly specific operating procedures and are subject to an hierarchical chain of command. This chain of command is supposed to ensure that the organization carries out the policy that is decided at the top, by the relevant political authority, board of directors or trustees. Democratic control of bureaucracies is supposed to be exercised mainly through their controlling bodies.

The attractions of bureaucracy are obvious enough. To the extent that it works according to rules, its operations are predictable and reliable in normal circumstances. A great deal of significant activity goes on without most of those who depend upon it having to worry about it. In so far as a bureaucracy is governed by a chain of command a policy formulated in fairly general terms is translated into ever more specific directives that result in a co-ordinated set of specific outputs giving effect to the policy. In the reverse direction the flow of information from the base operating agencies up through the system ensures that a large amount of material that is relevant to the assessment of policy is brought together as a basis for policy review. Bureaucracy, it might seem, is simply rational administration.

Actual bureaucracies are no doubt always imperfect, as are actual machines and organisms. But since organization is indispensable, so is bureaucracy, at least where there are permanent functions to be carried out and controlled. Permanent officers gain a great deal of experience that is indispensable to effective, predictable action, and are well motivated to make a success of their work in the hope of promotion and influence in the organization. Stable roles seem obviously important, and continuous monitoring of operations very much preferable to sporadic responses to breakdown in operations. Careful planning and co-ordinated implementation seems much more rational than *ad hoc* attempts to deal with problems as they arise. Whatever the defects of actual bureaucracies the remedy lies in better organization, better control, better flow of information and better policy. The widespread illusion that the upper levels of the pyramid are simply parasitic on the lower levels that produce tangible outputs is dangerous. Abolishing co-ordination and control would not make the lower levels more responsive to their clients, much less to the needs of the people as a whole. It would leave them with arbitrary and autarchic power. Abolishing bureaucracy would destroy in both public and private organizations significant economies of scale, the concentration of resources needed for important projects and the accumulation of information necessary to understand the impact of policy over a variety of sectors and over significant periods of time.

Against bureaucracy

The case against bureaucracy is equally well known. We have already mentioned some aspects of it. Simply because they work with a limited and entrenched repertoire of things that they can do bureaucracies are highly inflexible. The range of policy choices they can articulate is constricted by the sort of information they gather, the sort of failures or needs to which they normally respond and the sort of outputs that they are equipped to produce. They inhibit novel understanding, choice and action. The longer the chain of command the greater the distortion in the message that reaches the other end as at each level it is interpreted and translated into more specific terms and filtered by the bias, inertia and myopia prevalent at that level. The more the chains of command fan out the less likely are the interpretations put on the original directive to result in a set of specific activities that are even consistent, let alone integrated with each other. While the bureaucracy may monitor its own output, it will record that information in quantitative terms that have little regard to quality. The picture that is transmitted back up the line is almost always extremely misleading and very much filtered. The bureaucracy is almost always both incompetent and poorly motivated to assess the impact of its output on the needs and problems the output was intended to deal with. At the same time it is highly resistant to the use of other means to assess its performance.

However, a bureaucracy is not for most of the time engaged primarily in responding to directives. Each office is normally engaged in its routine work, in relative isolation both from its superiors and from other offices at the same level in the same department, let alone in other branches of the organization. In order to ensure the smooth operation of its routine it will tend to make itself as operationally self-sufficient as possible, often reduplicating services available elsewhere in the organization in order to avoid having to rely on 'outside' co-operation. Similarly, in order to be capable of responding to fluctuating demands on its services it will tend to try to hoard the resources to meet any eventuality, making 'busy' work of a routine kind to justify the need for them in times of slack demand. Notoriously, this functional tendency is reinforced by the anxiety of officers to increase the size and apparent importance of their empires. The result is not only a very uneconomic use of resources but a very cumbersome organization, almost incapable of responding appropriately to any actual demand for action.

Resources become locked into established agencies that are reluctant to make them available to other agencies, for fear of disturbing their routine, weakening their case for needing those resources, or losing functions to other agencies. Co-operation must be paid for, and the price is as high as the agency can exact. Policies that demand close and continuing co-operation of diverse agencies are inherently very difficult to implement and even more difficult to assess when they fail. Reorganizing the chain of command is the usual response to such failures. New agencies are set up, old ones transferred to new organizational locations, responsibilities redefined in order to avoid a repetition of the same situation. But already the situation has changed and the new organization has not anticipated the change.

One could go on detailing the inherent problems of bureaucracy. Even most bureaucrats do not like it very much. They feel constrained by all those rules even when they are seen as having great power.

Minimizing bureaucracy

No doubt a certain amount of bureaucracy is necessary, since some permanent and centralized agencies of substantial size are necessary in a highly complex society. The question is whether it can be minimized. Two ways have been suggested, market control and political decentralization. I shall return to the question of the market in the next chapter. Let us assume for the moment that a large range of public goods cannot be supplied by the market but only by politically, preferably democratically, controlled organizations. Two questions then arise: (1) Is it practicable to break down agencies providing public goods into units that are small enough to enjoy a relatively short chain of command, granted the need for reliability, co-ordination and adequacy to meet very broad social problems? (2) Is there a feasible way of ensuring democratic control over such autonomous specialized agencies? This latter question is, I believe, the crucial one. It will take up a great deal of the rest of this book. Meanwhile, it is important to face the first question.

It is obvious that there is no difficulty in principle about devolving autonomy to smaller units. It is a principle of bureaucratic organization that the operating agencies in an organization should, as far as possible, each be autonomous within its special domain. The various agencies in a bureaucracy are usually not primarily instruments of a higher purpose but operating bodies with regular direct responsibilities to various clients to whom they respond. Some of those clients may be other agencies rather than the public. Even so, the realtionship will frequently not be one of detailed subordination in operation, even if the agency was set up by its client. In an administrative structure, unless function overrides status, chaos will ensue. The stability of modes of operation, the attention to detail and clear definition of responsibilities that are conditions of a successful operation, presuppose the principle of subordinate autonomy, even in organizations as tightly hierarchical as an army.

There is no inherent difficulty in specifying and giving autonomy to various functions even when these functions are highly interdependent. On the contrary, a function that depends on another usually needs to be able to rely on that function being carried out without its having to do anything to ensure that it is. For the most part diverse independent agencies rely on higher levels of the bureaucratic hierarchy not to ensure that there is some explicit co-ordination of the agencies on which they depend, but simply to ensure that those agencies do their proper jobs. Is bureaucratic oversight a better means of ensuring that organizations do their jobs properly than direct democratic control?

The question of control

For there to be democratic control the members of the controlling body should be representative of those with a stake in
the good performance of the functions they are superintend-
ing, and should understand the problems involved in carrying
them out. The question then is how to ensure that people of
this sort are appointed. But even granting that this problem
can be solved, the defenders of bureaucracy will still raise
objections. The most important is that a controlling body of
this sort is much more likely than a bureaucratic superior to
negate the proper autonomy of the agency it controls. The
bureaucratic superior has usually been through the ranks and
knows from experience and training the importance of
autonomy. Moreover, officialdom can resist pressures to
intervene in *ad hoc* ways much more easily than representatives that are beholden to particular interests that are
affected by the agency's operations. The higher official can
be and is motivated to take a broader and longer-term point
of view than a committee representing interested parties.

It is easy enough to dismiss the bureaucrat's defence in the
name of popular sovereignty and to raise counter-objections
based on the tendency of higher-level bureaucrats to protect
their empires from scrutiny of any sort. The bureaucrat is
also subject to pressures that have little to do with the welfare
of the clients that the office serves. Promoting ease of
administration, the appearance of efficiency, loyalty to the
department and the interests of his or her immediate
superiors are some of these pressures. Even a bureaucrat's
genuine concern for the welfare of the agency's clients is inevitably paternalistic, shaped by his or her conception of
what is needed rather than by what the clients want, much
less really need.

Nevertheless the bureaucrat's objections to democratic
control raise a crucial point. It is desirable that the controllers
should have direct knowledge of and interest in the needs the

agency is intended to serve. It is not desirable that they each conceive their task simply as one of maximizing the pay-off to his or her particular constituency in the short term. They need to be motivated to seek to build up the agency and direct its policies in such a way that the long-term interests of all concerned will be maximized, often at some cost to a number of quite powerful short-term interests. It is a crucial test of any proposal for democratic control that it can give a plausible solution to this problem. If not we may be forced to accept a fairly high level of bureaucracy. A local health clinic, for example, will prefer to be subject to predictable regulation by a bureaucracy rather than constant unpredictable interference by people who are more concerned to show off their power and concern than to understand the problems of running a clinic and contribute constructively to solving them.

The difficulty might seem to be compounded when there is a need for explicit co-ordination and co-operation between various agencies to carry out projects and broad social programmes that transcend the functions of any one of them. It is important to my case to argue that this difficulty is less troublesome than it might appear. It has two aspects, one that might be called a technical one, concerned with joint planning and execution of specific projects, and a social policy one, concerned with questions about directions of social change. They involve very different considerations. The technical question turns on a comparison between largely voluntary co-operation between distinct agencies and largely enforced co-operation in a bureaucratic structure. The policy question is a matter of the ways in which decisions are to be reached about social priorities and how those decisions are to be fed into the planning process.

Co-ordination and co-operation

The technical question is the more easily answered. If the control of each of the various bodies that are involved in

some community project such as the development of a new
housing estate is vested in a committee that represents community interests, co-operation is likely to be very much easier
than between the distinct agencies under a variety of bureaucratic controls. Standing departmental rivalries, fears of 'outside' interference, red tape of all kinds and the inertia of
routine are much less likely to be in evidence. Particular projects can be originated from a variety of different sources,
and the ones that will win out are those supported by the
widest consortia of agencies concerned. The detailed planning and execution of particular projects can be handled by
co-ordinating committees. There would, no doubt, be a need
for recognized arbitrators with authority to determine issues
that were deadlocked between agencies, but these would have
no authority to intervene until negotiation between the parties broke down. How such machinery might work and what
authority it would have I shall show in more detail in a later
chapter.

The mirage of policy

The policy problem is much more difficult to answer, if only
because it is much more elusive. The full answer to it can
emerge only when we have thought through the whole matter
of democracy in a radically new way. At this stage what needs
to be challenged is the question itself. On most issues there is
no problem of policy. The illusion that there is is an artefact
of our present forms of government. It is true, of course, that
even in the richest societies there are choices to be made between priorities among desirable objectives, discriminations
to be made between desirable and undesirable forms of social
development and between different long-term courses of action. But it is almost wholly misleading to think of social construction and change in terms of the progressively more
detailed application of high-level principles and objectives to
every more concrete circumstances either by processes of

choosing means to ends, or by ways of instantiating general ideas. The importance that this image of social policy-making has assumed is due almost completely to the centralized character of the state bureaucracy and the peculiarities of the electoral process. Political parties attempt to persuade the electors that in voting they are deciding between rival social policies. That is a contention I shall examine later on.

In fact there are issues of broad social policy that are vitally important, but our present electoral systems are powerless to deal with them. At the level of decision between different constructive projects, however, questions of policy are largely irrelevant. What matters are the likely effects of the various practical schemes and their incidence on the various groups of people affected by them. The problem is to make best use of existing resources to produce the whole gamut of results that are desirable in different ways and degrees. As I shall argue in more detail later, there can be no golden rule here that can be applied to assess which is the best proposal. The important point for our present purposes, however, is that it is very often much easier to get agreement about which solution to a given problem is best in the circumstances than it is to get soundly based agreement on a comprehensive policy that purports to supply a general criterion of what is best.

A viable policy presupposes that the policy-makers have a very sound idea of what things can be done, on what scale and in what areas, given the resources available. Policy that is not based on such information is merely a recipe for a mixture of failures and missed opportunities. Too many projects are promoted because they purport to be in line with slogans, or left undone simply because they are not.

In originating, elaborating and securing support for specific projects that make maximum use of the resources available to meet the real needs of those affected, consortia of agencies in direct contact with the specific resources and needs in question are likely to be more effective than relatively inflexible and remote bureaucracies. They may lack the permanently installed experts and planners that a bureaucracy comprises, but it is usually more efficient to hire teams of such experts for specific projects than to be saddled with the limited capacities of permanent officers. Obviously such a practice permits of much greater experimentation and innovation. It also cuts down standing overheads. Policy assessments in most cases cannot consist of sets of fixed priorities. Any practical decision between competing proposals has to be based on attempts to quantify the relative costs and benefits involved. A reasonable and responsive policy will emerge from such a consideration of competing proposals, if those making the assessments are guided by specific knowledge of and sensitivity to the real needs of those affected.

In so far as there are policy questions of a more general sort, questions about the overall balance of different kinds of projects and the general emphasis of development, it is undesirable that these be handled bureaucratically. Ideally speaking, in our present parliamentary systems these are matters for political parties, the cabinet, the legislature and specific political appointees. It is notorious, of course, that these political agencies are not very successful in imposing on the bureaucracies the emphases and orientations they favour. Nevertheless, one of the most difficult tasks that the advocate of decentralization has to face is just this deeply rooted conviction that it ought to be possible for the popular will to express itself by imposing policy on the 'public service' through centralized organs of political decision-making. It is widely believed, especially by those who favour social change, that strong centralized political control is a necessary condition of coherent change. Even those who recognize that bureaucracies are very difficult to control and biased in favour of the status quo are inclined to believe that weakening the power of central government inevitably gives more power to existing interests.

Varieties of decentralization

The short answer to these contentions is that the result of weakening centralized authority depends entirely on what other authorities take up its functions. In this case it is a question of how political priorities can be articulated and expressed in the community as a whole. The positive solution of this problem will engage us in later chapters. In the present context, I want to emphasize only one crucial point. I agree that devolving the functions of central government down to smaller local units of *generalized* political decision-making, states, provinces, counties or municipalities, or leaving them to the 'private sector', does tend to transfer power to entrenched interests. The alternative I am elaborating is quite different. It is a matter of giving autonomy to highly *specialized* agencies, many of which would have a limited geographical scope, though a number would be national or international. The point is to break down comprehensive political power at each and every level.

How this is possible remains to be shown. The present point is that if it *is* possible centralized bureaucracies are not necessary for carrying out public projects. The need for centralized bureaucracy is wholly a result of the alleged need for centralized political control. It is a functional necessity of the state, not a functional necessity of any kind of constructive activity.

II PRIVATE BUREAUCRACIES

The corporation

It is not only states that generate bureaucracies. The growth of state bureaucracies has been paralleled by a comparable growth of large privately owned corporations, and, in some countries, of publicly owned corporations that operate in the market in much the same way as the private ones. Such corporations are responsible in some degree to their shareholders, whether these be individual investors, other companies or the state. It is clear that this responsibility is mainly limited to their paying some reasonable dividend to shareholders and building up their assets. Normally shareholders can neither have nor aspire to have any significant say in the corporation's activities, except in those cases where the corporation is effectively a subsidiary of some very powerful shareholder with other interests which it helps to promote.

As for the general public, it can put some constraints on what corporations can do by using state power, but any influence that it has on the positive direction of corporations is exercised through the market place, and such pressure as consumer groups and special interest groups can use to affect the corporation's reputation. The large corporation is, by and large, very stable, highly autonomous and largely self-financing, growing mainly from retained profits rather than new capital. At first sight, then, it seems to be a very efficient form of organization, well adapted to its environment. It is also very powerful. In the market place it can and often does exercise monopolistic or oligopolistic power, setting and maintaining prices, effectively excluding outsiders from entering the market and exercising a very strong influence on the pattern of life of both consumers and its own workers. Through its economic power it can also exercise great influence on government decisions.

The apoligists for large corporations sometimes make much the same claims on their behalf as are made for government bureaucracies. They are agencies of rational, long-term, and relatively enlightened planning. They can muster the resources to bring about major productive undertakings, exploit economies of scale and introduce stability and predictability to key sectors of economic life. To some limited extent these contentions are correct. As in the case of government bureaucracies the question is whether these advantages could not be secured in other ways and whether they are not over-whelmingly outweighed by other considerations. The only additional features of the private corporations that are alleged in their favour by comparison with government bureaucracies relate to their dependence on the market. The market forces on the private corporation a concern for efficiency, as well as a responsiveness to the needs of consumers and a readiness to innovate that has no parallel in the public sector. It is forced into these concerns in its own interest, but ultimately they are also in the public interest. The validity of these claims will be examined when we come to examine the market mechanism. In any case they are not arguments for size. On the contrary, the larger the corporation the less tightly is it governed by market constraints.

In the case of the so-called conglomerates, such as ITT, which control a great variety of companies with no functional relationship between their operations, one of their main purposes is to insulate the component companies from certain effects of the market. In particular, they can raise capital more cheaply, pool reserves and assist each other in ways that would not be possible without central co-ordination. Their viability has nothing to do with any increase in productive efficiency or even marketing, but only with the business of monetary management. Even in the case of single-industry giants such as the car manufacturers, the structure of the corporation has more to do with making money than making cars. All such manufacturers buy in substantial quantities of components because it is more efficient to do so. That they seek to expand their capacity to produce most of the components themselves is more a matter of securing their independence from outside supplies and their ability to keep potential competitors out of the industry than of technical desirability. It is also, of course, a matter of building up the capital assets of the corporation and the power of those who control it.

The market simplifies control of the organization

The corporation that acts for profit in the market place is in a very much simpler position for monitoring its impact and efficiency than a public corporation. Its impact is measured by its share of the market and its efficiency by its profitability. These measures of success can be applied directly to most operating divisions by comparing the costs of one division with another or with the costs of buying in various products from outside. Because they are subject to such clear and inexorable judgement divisional managers can be given a much freer hand than in a bureaucracy producing public goods. Empire building, lack of responsiveness to needs and opportunities, and sheer laziness show up sooner and much more clearly and quickly in falling sales and profits than in public dissatisfaction. Precisely because there is always a great deal of public dissatisfaction it is extremely difficult to distinguish clear messages from the general noise.

It is because of these advantages that private bureaucracies have a much better reputation than public ones. Their power is often feared, but their efficiency is less frequently questioned. Nevertheless, they are inefficient when it comes to innovation. New products, and technical and productive revolutions tend to come from small firms. There is an inherent tendency for large firms to entrench existing technical practice in an organizational structure that is not easily changed, to concentrate on marginal improvements in current practice rather than radical rethinking, to attempt to persuade consumers to buy what the corporation is geared to produce rather than explore new needs and new ways of meeting them, to economize by squeezing suppliers, workers and retailers rather than by radical re-organization.

Much more will have to be said about efficiency in allocation of resources and in responding to needs when we come to criticize the market mechanism. Meanwhile, I want to examine a number of questions about industrial democracy, assuming for the moment that the market mechanism is an inadequate form of popular control over large productive enterprises. I shall also assume that the point of industrial democracy is not primarily to enhance the interests of people as consumers, or even to protect their common interest in their material heritage of natural and produced resources, but to give greater scope for all-round development of people's capacities and social relations by giving them more control over and responsibility for their work.

Obviously, advocates of industrial democracy often want to argue that there is no systematic conflict between these objectives, and even that each reinforces the other. But their central case rests on the inherent desirability of enhancing the satisfaction people get out of their work, simply because it is so substantial a part of their lives. Sacrificing satisfaction in one's work for the sake of leisure activities is to be avoided if possible. The desirable thing is to break down the work-leisure dichotomy.

Industrial democracy and control

It is by no means clear exactly what the members of a work team need to control or participate in to get satisfaction from their work. Discharging the tasks of management is itself difficult work, and not everybody finds it congenial. By and large we enjoy doing those things we are good at doing, and aptitudes for negotiation, persuasion, policy decision and administration are as unevenly distributed as aptitudes for scientific experimentation, theorizing, playing the piano or any craft skill. Doctrines that claim that the proper development of human personality is possible only if all these rational capacities are developed to the full in every person are essentialist, dogmatic and ultimately repressive. They attempt to force people into a single mould. They arouse little enthusiasm in most workers because they implicitly devalue other talents. Indeed, the main attraction of proposals for participatory democracy is their opposition to the prevailing practices that tend to assign workers narrowly circumscribed roles and very little autonomy within those roles. Such interest as most workers have in having a say in management is related to defence of their jobs and conditions of work. By and large they prefer to have these interests defended by a special independent organization, the trade union, and fear that co-option of their representatives into the tasks of management will blunt their effectiveness in advancing the specific interests of workers. Yugoslav theory and experience of management elected by workers attests to these points.[2] There have been strikes in worker-controlled enterprises.

A fairly sharp distinction and tension between management and labour is inevitable in a market economy where the success of a firm is crucially dependent on risk-taking decisions about the mix and quantity of production, pricing, contracts with suppliers and retailers, and the constant monitoring of costs. Nor can analogous risks and problems be avoided in a non-market economy. Ultimately the fate of the enterprise will be judged by its usefulness in the plan, and management decisions will be taken in the light of the needs of the plan rather than the preferences of the workers. Management would like to put the brunt of the risks on to workers, workers to insist that the firm must accept them.

Even if there were some way in which the workers could have an effective and relatively direct participation in these decisions, another problem emerges. If workers can change jobs easily there is little incentive for them to place the long-term viability of the enterprise before their own short-term interests. If they cannot easily change jobs they do not have one of the most effective ways of both securing work that suits them and ensuring that work that is generally regarded as unpleasant is compensated adequately by other rewards. From this point of view it is probably more important for the welfare of workers both individually and collectively that they have a positive freedom to choose what jobs they will accept than that they enjoy either security of employment in a particular job or responsibility for the way that enterprise is managed.

Freedom to work or not

Such freedom depends on a host of factors such as support while they are looking for a job, opportunities for retraining, portability of entitlements such as superannuation and leave, and in some cases assistance with the costs of moving themselves and their families. Ideally, perhaps, nobody would be compelled legally or economically to work, at least for most of the time. In such a situation people would only work because of the intrinsic rewards and the goods and services they could purchase with additional income. It sounds utopian. However, it is a striking fact that most people who are rich enough to live at least moderately comfortably on their unearned incomes do undertake full-time jobs. Many women who are under no social or economic pressure to work look for outside employment when there is not enough interesting work at home. If the opportunities for interesting work and the rewards for uninteresting work were greater there is little reason to doubt that most people would want to work. In such circumstances, given modern productivity, advanced societies (and very soon not so advanced ones) could afford to carry those who, whatever their reasons, did not want to work, and were content with a minimal income. The cost would be the price of ensuring that work would be freely undertaken.

In such a situation the problems of participation might be expected to be solved in a very large variety of ways, depending on specific contracts of employment between individuals and teams of workers and management, however management is chosen and whatever the criteria of success for the enterprise. Such a system should be efficient, flexible and dynamic, if only it could be financed and administered satisfactorily. A host of questions arise. Who is going to decide on the level of payments to those who do not work? Is the money to come from taxation on those who do work, or is there some better way of raising it? Does it not in any case require a very powerful state apparatus of the kind we have already rejected? The answers to these questions are complex and will, I hope, emerge in the course of subsequent chapters. At the same time I shall attempt to produce reasons for thinking that a social structure based on negotiated arrangements between genuinely autonomous groups can better satisfy the conflicting requirements of libertarian and socialist aspirations than any form of capitalism or of planned economy. Finally, as this is not just a conceptual exercise, I shall try to show that the solutions I am advocating could work under social conditions that either exist or could be brought about by means that are already available. All that is lacking is the political will.

III CONTROL, COMMAND AND SERVICE

Varieties of organization and control

There is great danger in talking of bureaucracy that the enormous variety of kinds of organization is lost from view. So far we have concentrated on productive agencies that deliver positive services to consumers such as public utilities, educational institutions, hospitals and the like. At the other end of the spectrum purely regulatory agencies are concerned only with keeping the activities they regulate within certain bounds, for example, police, safety and pollution control authorities. But many agencies have mixed roles, or play one kind of role as a means to another. So a consumer protection agency may, in order to carry out its regulatory role, produce a great deal of information that is useful to other agencies and to individuals for a variety of purposes.

One of the things that people most frequently complain about when they object to bureaucracy is the rigidity and arbitrariness of its control functions, the impenetrable thicket of rules and regulations, the ways in which rules are applied, the counter-productive character of the rules, the amount of work that goes into getting permissions and making reports. All of this makes it unnecessarily difficult and costly to do many things that are otherwise needed or useful, and it is open to both a host of petty abuses and some significant major abuses. Hence the very widespread belief that it would be much better if productive organizations could be so designed that they were as nearly self-regulating as possible.

In order to understand the possibilities of self-regulation it is important to look more closely at the differing kinds of control that are involved in organizations of a relatively permanent sort. It has become fashionable to use the word 'control' in an increasingly abstract way, which in turn relates to very vague conceptions of power, authority and agency. Take, for example, the dining room of a large hotel. From one point of view it might be said to be under the control of the customers. Individually they give the 'orders' that determine what is produced when and in what quantities. Collectively they establish the pattern of demand and constrain the operators to meet that pattern. At the other end of the operation the hotel management controls what is done. It not only sets policy and decides what resources are to be put into these operations but monitors them through its accounting procedures and quality control. In between, the restaurant manager controls the actual production, assigning responsibilities to cooks, waiters and other staff, determining the menu and supervising every aspect of the operation.

It is obvious enough that each of those controls serves a different specific set of interests in the operation, each operates by very different mechanisms and each requires different knowledge and skills. A similar structure of different kinds of control is evident in most government departments. Policy is set at the top, resources assigned and monitoring procedures set up. Precise regulations are made, procedures of implementation and assignments of responsibilities instituted by permanent officers within the organization. The activities of clerks at their desks and officers in the field are controlled by clients with claims or by delinquents to be brought into line. From this point of view the police are 'controlled' by criminals and the army by the enemy.

In addition to these 'vertically' differentiated controls, there are usually a variety of 'horizontal' controls. The firm is controlled by its competitors, the government department by its rivals within the bureaucracy that want to take over its functions or resources. Most organizations are sensitive to fashion, the approval or disapproval of opinion-makers. Their professional standing is not only a means to whatever other ends the organization or its members may have, but puts the seal on the intrinsic worth of what they are and what they do. What these horizontal controls are worth as controls depends largely on the appropriateness and openness of the competition through which they exert their effects. Those who articulate the verdicts must be governed by solid, adequate information and appropriate criteria of assessment. They must not be manipulated by public relations exercises, bemused by their own capacity to orchestrate public opinion, or in the service of extrinsic purposes.

For many purposes avoiding the undesirable aspects of bureaucracy is mainly a matter of substituting horizontal for vertical controls both within the organization and over the organization. Horizontal controls, especially peer assessments, can be much more flexible and much more apt to produce excellent performances and readiness to take proper risks than any controls that can be exercised from above or below. Assessment from below is necessarily largely assessment on results, especially unpalatable results. The consumer, the lay person, cannot know whether an organization is making the most of the opportunities available or is technically efficient. The public may not know what it is missing. Even where it does, it can voice its discontents only in negative terms.

Control from above is even more unsatisfactory. The further it is away from the ultimate product the less it can assess accurately its quality and appropriateness. The further away it is from the ultimate production process the less it is in a position to be aware of or appreciate alternative possibilities. The more tightly it attempts to control the organization the more it becomes a prisoner of its subordinate command structure. The more it has to rely on negative sanctions, the greater the emphasis it puts on mere quantity, regularity and avoidance of error rather than quality, adaptability and experiment.

Increasing horizontal control, however, presupposes not only dismantling control from above but ensuring that the legitimate need for control can be met. In order to understand this problem better it is useful to distinguish two aspects of organizations that are not usually contrasted strongly enough. Take an extreme case, an army. One purpose that control and central planning must serve is to ensure that the army is well prepared to meet a variety of contingencies. It must be kept functioning, and occupied in a host of day-to-day activities when it is not fighting. It must be equipped, organized, trained and exercised on a continuing basis. At the other extreme when it is actually engaged in warfare it must respond to a variety of different demands in a flexible, prompt and effective way. As a standing peacetime army it is organized by regulation, budgeting, long-term programmes and established routines. As a combat unit it is deployed by command, leadership, co-operative action and detailed response to the contingencies of battle.

Readiness and performance

Every organization has these two aspects to some degree, often involving different systems of control. The organic analogies are striking. One system (or complex of systems) builds up our muscles, keeps them in dynamic equilibrium and repairs them. Another puts them into action. The normal administrative apparatus of an organization ensures its supply and general preparedness to produce a certain sort of performance by regular standardized routines. The specific controls that bring about particular performances may come through quite distinct channels. Even when they come through the 'normal' channels they take a different form, orders of all sorts, decision-making conferences between various units, and specific programmes rather than rules, routine checking or standing instructions.

It is relatively easy to monitor and assess particular performances. The results are often unequivocal and the relations between the decisions and those results easy to trace. Horizontal controls are usually prominent and powerful in such cases. But what an organization can do in response to specific and episodic demands on it depends on the soundness of its preparation and the range of its repertoire of performances. These things are very much harder to assess prior to any actual performance. The preparations may be irrelevant to the challenge that in fact emerges. It is often said that armies are usually prepared to fight the last war rather than the next. The same tends to apply to large organizations generally. Their very success in building up a capacity for production and action of a certain kind makes it difficult for them to do anything else. They build in so many constraints on variety and initiative precisely because they are well designed and integrated to produce certain results and not others.

Formalized horizontal controls are not likely to be very much better than vertical ones in this respect. The standards of sound practice are inevitably conservative and conventional. There is, in fact, as the advocates of 'free enterprise' have so insistently reminded us, no solution to these problems in terms of planning and control. If we are going to have productive organizations that are innovative, risk-taking and easily changed, they must be controlled mainly by inducing those who direct them to face the risk of failure in the hope of the rewards of success. Individuals and organizations must have access to the resources necessary to experiment. To deter recklessness they must pay a penalty for failure. To motivate them to try they must receive rewards for success. The criteria of success must be appropriate and they must be applied appropriately. Assessment must be directed mainly at performance rather than at preparations for performance.

If that is the case, then there is not much hope for the army. The proponents of 'free enterprise' are equally certain that there is no hope for public enterprise either. The crucial problem, assuming for the moment that success and failure can be assessed and rewarded appropriately, is the allocation of resources to individuals and groups that want to experiment. It seems fairly obvious that these will have to be distributed in fairly small parcels. The larger the stake in proportion to the total resources available the less sense it makes to encourage risk-taking. The larger the scale of the experiment the more likely it is to exclude undertaking other experiments with which it might be compared. The larger the organization the more it is likely to become inert or inflexible.

On the other hand, the larger the number of organizations competing to supply a similar service the more difficult it is to decide which are to get the chance to do so, the more likely it is that there will be duplication, overlapping and pointless competition between them. Co-ordination, negotiation and stable joint enterprises are the more difficult the more independent sources there are of variation and aim between the agencies whose co-operation is needed for a given project. Where one is not relying on the market, which distributes resources mainly on the basis of past success in the market, it is difficult to see how one escapes the need for a centralized bureaucracy to make the distribution.

There are formidable problems. The solution that I shall advocate is in principle very simple. We shall come to it in due course. For the moment I shall try to clear the ground a little more.

Power and responsibility

One of the paradoxes of bureaucracy is that it is generally perceived as powerful and oppressive by its clients while those who work in it at all levels see themselves powerless and burdened with responsibilities. The paradox is, of course, easily resolved. The bureaucrat is perceived as having great power because he or she is in a position to invoke a complex of regulations, provisions, procedures and requirements that impose burdens on clients, structure very tightly the choices open to clients and bring great pressure on them to act or refrain from acting contrary to the bureaucrat's desires. The bureaucrat is harassed by the pressures from above, below and each side to make rules and practices work in spite of their being ill-designed to cope with circumstances that arise, and in spite of the failure of other parts of the machinery. The penalties for error and unauthorized behaviour are high, the rewards for success are low. That problems get solved is seen merely as fulfilling one's duties, even when the solving of them is in fact a result of great effort and ingenuity. In these circumstances there is a very strong temptation to fall back on a literal interpretation of instructions and regulations, to attempt to shift the locus of responsibility to somebody else and refuse to respond to substantive need whenever they threaten to create problems. It is very dispiriting.

There is no doubt that overcoming this paradox involves giving much greater freedom to those who are called on to solve the base level operating problems and much greater rewards for producing creative and beneficial solutions to them. This clearly involves more flexible controls, more attuned to substantive rather than procedural criteria. In general this is much easier to achieve when the context is one of meeting a substantial present challenge than in the regular context of maintaining an organization. An army in battle encourages initiative, even at the cost of bending the rules, calls for actions that are beyond the call of duty rather than routine compliance, and rewards the successful taking of risks. The contrast with regular discipline and management practices is as striking as the contrast in attitudes, behaviour and relationships among the participants in the two situations.

It is impossible, of course, to eliminate the routine work that is necessary to keep an organization functioning. Records must be kept, resources marshalled, training exercises repeated and structures maintained. By and large this 'housekeeping' work is much more tolerable if it is not an individual's or agency's unique occupation and if it can be seen as integral with and tailored to the requirements of substantive action by the agents themselves. So what is needed are small organizations that can be put together as occasion demands into more complex organizations, rather than large standing organizations from which units are dispatched to carry out particular tasks. The survival of any unit would be made to depend on its actual usefulness to its ostensible task and to other agencies, not just on the tendency of a large organization to hoard resources that might prove useful, and to multiply functions whose sole purpose is to keep the organization busy. In other words there needs to be a form of decentralization that puts resources in the hands of agents, gives them a flexible area of substantive responsibilities and rewards or penalizes them according to their success in discharging those responsibilities. Co-operation and co-ordination with other agencies must be included in those responsibilities and the manner and precise objectives of those joint efforts left to their initiative.

The terms of office of those who staff these agencies must be long enough for them to get to know the problems, evolve practicable solutions and carry through their projects to completion, but not long enough for them to sink into routine or prevent others from trying a fresh approach to the problems. The reward for success must be explicit recognition by their successors, clients and peers of the quality of their work. This would be expressed in part by a recognition of their suitability for tackling more difficult tasks, such as that of adjudicating conflicts between agencies, reviewing their structures and functions and allocating resources between them. Obviously, the key problem is making such a system work is, Who is to articulate the host of particular judgements of success and failure on which it depends and make and give effect to the consequent decisions?

Policy and control

It is obvious that such flexible organization, assuming it can work, could not be an effective instrument of any single narrowly defined policy, whether it be the military policy of a particular state, a definite centralized policy of income redistribution or the market strategy of a large corporation. It is designed to decentralize power and initiative and encourage experiment not just with means but with diverse specific goals. If there is some precise set of objectives that constitutes the will of the people it will not be an appropriate way of achieving them. On the other hand, if the will of the people is simply the very abstract objective that the best use be made of a great variety of community resources to do whatever can be done to meet the specific needs of many diverse, overlapping and dispersed groups of people, then it might be expected to be far more responsive, creative and effective in doing so than any centrally controlled bureaucracy.

It would not, however, be blind in the sense in which the market or an ecosystem is blind. Through such a system, I shall argue, much more dynamic and well-directed forms of social change would be possible than can be achieved by any form of centralized direction, however democratically controlled. If there were a widely shared view about the changes that need to be made in a society, it could articulate them in practice much more quickly, appropriately and effectively than any centralized process. As each agency in its own area of responsibility, and in co-operation with other agencies, attempted to advance those specific interests that were seen as disadvantaged, to give effect to those values that are most widely regarded as important and relative to their concerns, and to monitor and adapt their procedures in the light of their specific effects, the result should be a massive shift of policy.

Because the detailed implementation of policy would be so closely tied to specific problems and possibilities the danger of pure dogmatism and of systematically counter productive policies would be minimized. Entrenched interests that exercise great conservative force on a central government because of their ability to organize and concentrate their efforts on a large scale would usually be much less effective in dealing with a variety of autonomous specialized agencies. Even very powerful local interests that can dominate a centralized local authority would find it harder to dominate a variety of specialized authorities many of which had no narrowly local base or little organic connection with the activities in which the local interest was based.

Conditions of decentralization

The sort of social organization I am advocating would itself constitute a major change, one of the most significant in history. Nevertheless, although the problems of introducing it and making it work in practice may seem insurmountable, many of the social conditions of its working are already present in most advanced polyarchies and in the major socialist countries. People are very well aware of the enormous complexity of such societies. There is a very strong desire to dismantle centralized controls and disperse power to functionally appropriate units. In spite of all that has been said about the 'privatization' of life as people have become aware of their powerlessness, there is a great interest in public affairs and, I believe, great willingness to participate in them if only it were more possible to do so in some limited but effective way. The interests of most people are sufficiently various for them to be well aware that their overall interests in a complex society can be advanced only by constructive co-operation. They resort to confrontation reluctantly, as a last resort. They are well aware that a great deal of the avoidable evil in the world is the result not of malevolence but of agents being forced into inappropriate policies and actions by the requirements of their institutional roles. Even where malevolence is to blame, that it can have such disastrous effects is the result of institutions that make it possible for such people to acquire inordinate power.

Indeed it is remarkable that public and private bureaucracies in many countries function as well as they do in spite of their rigidity, their tendency to produce misinformation, their costliness and the lack of satisfaction of both their staff and their clients. It is, I believe, very good evidence that there are many people in such organizations who are prepared to work very hard to get the appropriate things done, to respond imaginatively to crises and to work for the public welfare as they understand it. That so many people are prepared to put up with the degree of bureaucratic control that they do, and with the very high taxation necessary to fund it, is evidence of a realism that is prepared to accept considerable costs to achieve social goods that are not necessarily in their own interests narrowly conceived. Many people vote for parties that will tax them more severely than their competitors because they are more concerned about the direction of social policy than about the cost or benefits to them individually in the short run.

Of course, people who would derive satisfaction from working for the public good for modest but solid rewards may be a relatively small minority. Nevertheless, they can be found in pretty well any section of the community, whether one divides it up by occupation, status or region. They crop up all over the place. It is not necessary to preach some narrow morality that exalts such people above those whose interests are more private or more special. All that is required is that most people recognize that public service is *a* worthy thing, along with devotion to one's artistic talent or one's family or science or dahlias. Much less is it necessary or desirable to attempt to mould everybody into a public person. Why should not those who are not interested in public office simply turn over the work to those who are, provided they are so organized and chosen as to be sensitive to the interests that need to be taken into account and adequately motivated to do a good job?

The result would be democratic if all interests were appropriately represented, if everybody who wanted to had a reasonable and equal chance of participating actively and if no individual or group could acquire entrenched power in the system. Most of our lives depend on other people doing their jobs properly without our having any substantial control over what they do. We have to rely on others to do what needs to be done and absorb the effects as best we can. Many of those effects are in any case unpredictable and uncontrollable. The culture we share is the product of artists and scientists pursuing their own work. The opportunities for consumption we enjoy are the product of many independent producers attempting to produce things that they think people will want. The richness of our lives is in part at least the result of producers disconcerting our expectations, creating new challenges and opportunities for us, and inevitably certain disappointments. The morality to which we must adjust our personal relationships and the valuations people put on us are matters over which we can have only partial control. Social norms, our friends, and people's standards of judgement change in a variety of ways to which we have to respond.

For most people most public affairs are matters that they

can no more control than they can control the weather. They adjust to one as the other as best they can. They do not understand the complexities of public policy, and they know very well that their influence in such matters is in any case infinitesimal. They are prepared to accept any reasonable system for getting things done. Indeed they accept that there are plenty of people who know a lot better than what can be done and what results it is likely to have in most cases. However, even such people often have a strong interest in some area of public decision-making that affects them in a particular way, and they may well have or be prepared to acquire the skills and knowledge needed to take an active part in attempting to deal with that area. Given the opportunity they may make a significant contribution to it.

In the practical context of attempting to make decisions about complex matters such people are likely to learn that these questions are not zero-sum games where a gain for one interest is necessarily a loss for another. On the contrary most of them involve a variety of dimensions in each of which various interests are advantaged or disadvantaged in different ways. The optimal solution results from a process of constructive trading in which the significance of losses and gains changes with the context set by other aspects of a proposal taken as a whole. In such a situation the ones who are likely to win are those who best understand what others have at stake and are able to articulate proposals that meet a wide variety of interests in various ways to a degree that is satisfying to each.

Such bargaining is impossible if everybody affected is supposed to participate. It is necessarily a matter for small numbers of people who are prepared to put in a great deal of work on it. They must not be too narrowly constrained by 'non-negotiable' demands. They must rely to a large extent on their knowledge not just of what those they represent want, but of what they need and what they might reasonably be expected to settle for. The question then is how can we get this sort of negotiation into the hands of people who can be trusted to do their best for the interests they are supposed to represent? The almost universally accepted answer is by free, openly contested elections. Our next task is to show that that answer is radically unsatisfactory.

3
Democracy and representation

I VOTING

Most contemporary authors explicitly or implicitly treat free elections for the supreme offices in the state as a defining characteristic of democracy. By contrast, I shall argue that electoral systems are inimical to rule by the people for the people. In order to bring this out it is necessary to look closely at what voting can achieve, what alternatives might be envisaged in the abstract and what are the conditions under which they might produce acceptable results.[1]

Revealing preferences

Theorists of voting who have used the tools of economic analysis have been much troubled by the problem of how to get individuals to reveal their preferences. Let us grant, just for the sake of argument, that people have a consistent and complete set of definite preferences ranging over all the alternatives available in a given context of decision, and that each voter (person or institution) knows what its preferences are. There is quite literally a problem about getting people to reveal those preferences in many voting situations where it pays to conceal them for strategic reasons. But the more fundamental problem is, How *can* votes express preferences? What the economists work with are indifference curves that represent a set of trade-offs between costs and benefits.

People's preferences are expressed by the relative *prices* they are prepared to pay for a certain additional amount of each specific good. But voting rarely expresses a clear willingness to pay *any* definite price for any definite good. The act of voting is almost costless. The cost of getting what I vote for is often shifted on to somebody else. Again, my voting for rather than against does not say how strongly I am in favour of a proposal. It cannot express anything like a price I am willing to pay. A majority with slight preferences one way may outvote almost as many strong preferences the other way. Moreover, voting is usually a matter of simply 'buying' or 'not buying' large packages, much of which one does not want. Mere voting tells us very little because it registers so little.

There might be a great deal to be said for people having to 'put their money where their mouth is', or, if not their money, since that is very unequally distributed, their time and effort. For example, one might acquire votes to be used as one sees fit by performing quanta of useful drudgery in approved public works. Voting would then measure the seriousness and strength of one's preferences. The difficulty is, of course, that few people would bother to acquire votes at any substantial cost if their votes had as little effect on the outcome as they normally must have in any large organization. Where there is a very large number of voters any individual's parcel of votes is unlikely to be significant. The larger the organization and the broader the issues presented to the voters the less likely is it that the outcome of voting will be translated into the sort of concrete output that any particular voter wants.

On the other hand, if the number of voters fell so dramatically that small numbers of votes were significant, such a system would encourage 'monomaniacs', those who were intensely devoted to a single issue. It is, of course, not too difficult to think up variants to guard against such dangers. For example, everybody might have a free vote on each question, and additional votes might be earned on a diminishing scale that made it costly to acquire a relatively large number of votes. Or there might be a limit on the number of votes that could be applied to a single issue. Again, various forms of trading in votes and proxies might be allowed under specific conditions, making it possible for the committed to acquire the votes of the indifferent by competing for them in some way.

The difficulty with all proposals that try to make voting a genuine expression of preferences by relating the act of voting to willingness to bear costs is that any given system of this sort will work only under a very narrow range of conditions. So as conditions change it will be necessary to make continuous adjustments to the system. Such changes inevitably favour some interests rather than others. An authority of sufficient integrity and ability to make these adjustments would have to be chosen on some other basis than the voting it is supposed to regulate. In any case there is no guarantee that there are solutions to many of these problems even in theory, let alone in practice.

Rationality and preferences

In practice people do not have definite preferences over the whole range of alternatives that affect them. They have neither the information nor the analytical skill nor the imagination to construct the sort of stable schedules that the economists' calculations require. They simply do not have the sort of preferences that economists want them to 'reveal'. What they usually have are a few likes and dislikes that are not systematically evaluated in relation to the feasible alternatives. To do that is, of course, a difficult thing, and often not worth our while. Of course, this applies to market transactions just as much as to voting. But there is a great difference. The market ultimately forces everybody into a set of precisely quantified bets about what will give them satisfaction. These bets are continuously readjusted in the light of experience. Many of them are related to very short-term outcomes. There is a tendency for the process of continual adjustments of expenditure to produce some sort of consistent allocation. Even so, a great many 'preferences' are stable simply because other alternatives have never been considered.

One may say, with some justification, that in such cases people prefer stability to any other advantages. In fact they often do, quite explicitly. But it is a completely blind preference when it consists in a refusal to contemplate alternatives. It does not consist in setting a finite price on the inconvenience of change. It is not a quantified factor among other factors but a refusal to quantify and calculate. So it is very misleading to argue that because such people pay a definite price for their 'choice', it does constitute a preference that is 'revealed' by the fact that the price is paid. The price that people in fact pay in such cases is not even evidence of a willingness to pay that price, since they may be quite unaware that they are paying what they are. Much less is it a guide to what they would be willing to pay if they knew. So people may stay on in a house as long as they can pay the rent, even though much more suitable accommodation could be found much more cheaply elsewhere, not because of any positive attraction to their present house, but simply to avoid having to contemplate change and the risks it involves. The avoidance of risk comes to have infinite weight.

In a changing world attempting to avoid risk by refusing to change oneself is not a rational strategy for *minimizing* risk. To forego all possibility of adapting oneself appropriately to changes one cannot control is to run a very substantial risk of being needlessly disadvantaged by those changes. Nevertheless many people do adopt such a strategy in practice for a host of bad reasons. They may be bewildered or paralysed by fear. They may trust in their luck or their patron saints. Often they are deprived of the time, information and assistance they would need even to contemplate the problem. Sometimes they are just stupid or lazy or perverse.

Where many of the preferences expressed in voting are of this nature there seems to be little point in trying to construct systems of voting that are based on taking them as rational preferences in the sense required by the model of rationality on which these constructions rest. It is like building a skyscraper out of any old materials that happen to turn up even though the design specifies materials of the highest quality.

It is important to avoid misunderstanding here. The argument is not that the wills of people who are irrational by some ideal measure should not be taken into account. It is not that it may not under some circumstances be expressed appropriately as a vote. The point is simply that there is no way of getting a set of precisely weighted preferences over a range of alternatives from a set of votes. They are not expressions of preferences in the required sense, since the value put on most of the alternatives is completely indeterminate or on others is fixed without any reference to their relative advantages and disadvantages.

It may be true that the market does in various ways put pressure on people to rationalize their preferences. In some sense most of us have to budget our money. But there is no way in which normal political processes force people to make realistic policy decisions between the range of alternatives open to them. There are just too many externalities, too many complications, and the time-scale is too long. If voting is to be a significant procedure in political decision-making it must be assigned a more modest role.

The limits of decision procedures

Even where there are genuine preferences there is no procedure, even in principle, by which all sets of expressed preferences can be aggregated into a social decision that guarantees an optimal solution to the task of reconciling them. There is a very substantial amount of precise knowledge about the theoretical impossibilities inherent in this kind of enterprise, especially since Kenneth Arrow discovered the 'Arrow barrier'.[2] It is very much less clear how relevant this knowledge is in a practical context. On the one hand, most social decision-making is at a level so far from the theoretical limits that those limits may well be as irrelevant to our purposes as absolute limits on the velocity of matter are to designers of motor cars. On the other hand, the most important practical difficulties are precisely those that are brushed aside in the theory, which tends to assume such conditions as perfect knowledge and rationality.

It is the practical problems that are most important in the present context. The work that has been done on theoretical models of the logic of preferences, voting and the conciliation of preferences makes several assumptions that are very unrealistic. One of these is that preferences between A and B are not affected by the outcome between, say, G and D. This assumption is necessary to ensure the transitivity of preferences, that is to say, that if A is preferred to B and B to C then A is preferred to C. The procedures of calculation require that we be able to construct alternatives that form constant and mutually independent objects of preference despite changes of context. However, in real life, states of affairs do not divide up so neatly. A conservative may prefer the status quo to a change B and B to a greater change C. Nevertheless, it may well be the case that in certain circumstances he or she would prefer the combination of C and D to A, believing, for example, that a radical, consistent and thoroughgoing change is preferable to an unstable, incoherent compromise.

Again, preferences often depend on a context of repetition. Apple pie may be my favourite dish, but I do not want it every night. There are, of course, ways of getting around such difficulties. In the limit one can exhibit the alternatives as a set of 'possible worlds' that conjointly exhaust all possible combinations of their components in every dimension in which they make a difference. The trouble is that the further one goes in that direction the further one departs from the original object of the exercise, namely to find a way of deriving an assessment of a complex from the assessments of its individual components or of comparing complexes on the basis of comparisons between their components taken discretely.

None of this is to say that there is no practical value at all in attempting to compare complex alternatives on the basis of preferences between their elements, but merely that such procedures are inconclusive. They may, for example, enable us to clarify why, although we prefer A to B and C to D we prefer B-with-D to A-with-C. The result may be a radical restructuring of our perceptions of the situation that is of the highest practical importance. On the other hand, it may well be that in a given context one gets a very good approximation to the actual range of relevant considerations by taking the elements as discrete, perhaps because the ways in which they are interrelated are so complex and variable that they can be taken as random for practical purposes. The point is that one cannot assume that they are random without some substantial warrant for doing so.

In general there are two possibilities. One can compare the results obtained by predicting people's preferences between aggregates on the basis of their preferences between the components of the aggregates with their actual choices between those aggregates and justify one's assumption that the conditions for applying this form of analysis are met by displaying its success in prediction.[3] Or one can attempt to show positively that the relations between the various alternatives are such that they cannot influence the aggregate result in any systematic way. The first method is unconvincing unless the number of cases in which success is demonstrated is large and homogeneous. It also supposes that we already possess a way of determining people's preferences between the aggregates that is independent of the method being tested. Normally that comes down to taking people's saying what they would prefer as an accurate guide to what they would in fact prefer. Since we cannot usually contrive test situations, we cannot test many predictions in fact. So the conditions under which such methods are reliable are themselves difficult to discover.

Attempting to demonstrate that there are no relevant factors that are omitted from a set of objects of choice is even more difficult. Even if there were some comprehensive theoretical framework that could ensure that the descriptions of the various alternatives were complete in some sense and independent of each other, it is doubtful whether this would help very much. It might be possible in principle to describe each alternative exhaustively in physical terms, but such descriptions would not bear any systematic relation to the description under which people form their preferences. These are irremediably subjective and intensional rather than objective and extensional.[4] It is not obvious, for example, that it is irrational to prefer object X to object Y that is an exact replica of X simply because X is a family heirloom.

These are only some of the difficulties in constructing a satisfactory formula for deriving preferences between aggregates from preferences between their components. If one adds them to the acknowledged difficulties of expressing weights of preferences in terms of votes, the problems of deriving satisfactory decisions by voting alone are clearly insurmountable in practice. That is the case even if we assume that people's preferences are consistent and well based. Obviously 'raw' preferences rarely are. We would all like to have incompatible things, sometimes because we are caught in unresolvable conflicts, sometimes because it is very difficult to know that they are incompatible. In these circumstances analyses of possible configurations of compatible preferences may be of great assistance in helping us determine the limits and sources of incompatibility and the ways in which we might revise our preferences to make them more realistic. But this use of preference theory is dialectical, involving a process of adjustment of preferences that undercuts any employment of preferences as fixed points of reference from which to derive a firm decision about a complex of preferences.

The practical importance of negotiations

In a social context, the only way in which this dialectical process can take place consciously is by negotiations in which the precise preferences of the participants are not fixed. Each party proposes to the other various packages, attempting to show how each might gain various advantages from alternatives that are also advantageous to their proponent. Very often such negotiations will involve key components that are in some degree prisoner's dilemma situations.[5] That is to say, the situation is so structured that the result of acting solely in one's own interest without regard to the actions of the other party will result in each preventing the other from getting what it wants. On the other hand, if each party is prepared to settle on a course of action that is less advantageous than that which it would prefer in the abstract, both can be assured of a result that is acceptable and in the circumstances the best attainable.

Clearly there are very tight limits on the number of parties that can enter into fruitful negotiations on any particular matter. A good deal of knowledge of the situation is required, a great deal of time must go into examining proposals and constructing counter-proposals, excluding irrelevancies and exploring possibilities. An enormous amount of information must be communicated to and assimilated by each participant. In practice negotiations tend to be expeditious and avoid cross purposes and irrelevancies to the extent that the parties come to know each other well enough to reach a number of tacit agreements about what does not need to be spelled out explicitly, what is not negotiable, what is impracticable and so on. It is also desirable, though not, of course, necessary, that the parties are in a position to trust one another to work for a genuinely optimal solution rather than attempt to conceal relevant information or deceive the other parties to the negotiations.

The result of these considerations applied to any reasonably complex society is that there is no possibility of reaching reasonable conclusions about matters in which a diversity of interests and opinions are involved by voting or by the direct involvement of all those affected by the decisions. Most decisions have to be left to negotiators who enjoy a very large margin of discretion about what to concede and what to refuse to other parties. Realistically, then, the problem of democracy is that of selecting and controlling the representatives who are to negotiate the various decisions that have to be made about matters of public policy and administration.

Referendums

There is, however, another procedure that is rarely used but sometimes advocated to ensure democratic control over negotiations, namely that the final package constructed by the negotiators should be submitted to the vote of the people affected by it. This happens regularly within bodies such as parliaments where subcommittees report and recommend but the whole body accepts or rejects their proposals. Occasionally even bodies that have the power to act submit proposals to general referendums of those they represent, as the British parliament did in the case of entry into the European Economic Community. Some argued in that particular case that parliament was evading its responsibility. Its proper function is to decide what is best for the nation, which is not necessarily what a majority will vote for.

Whatever the merits of that particular case, there are sound reasons for not regarding referendums on specific proposals as a satisfactory way of controlling public policy in most instances and as a general practice. Some derive fairly directly from points we have already made about voting. On any specific issue it is very likely that many groups of people and interests will be affected much more strongly than others. Equity would seem to require that they be given votes in proportion to the degree in which they are affected. Otherwise a relatively apathetic majority may block a proposal that is of great advantage to a minority simply out of distaste for change or because it involves some relatively trivial adjustment on their part. But of course such uneven distributions of interest vary widely from issue to issue. Determining the relevant voting structure for each issue would be, to say the least, extremely difficult.

Moreover, it is often the case that a relatively small deliberative body will take a much more enlightened view on a matter than the general public does, even when it is a matter in which most people have something approaching an equal interest. Penal policy, and particularly capital punishment, is a case in point. Not many people understand a great deal about criminology. It is not necessary to attribute to them irrational motivations or moral insensitivity to understand why they often support capital punishment even when their legislature does not. They are using oversimplifed analyses of the problem, often based on very unusual cases. Their judgement is not soundly based.

It might well be that if referendums on issues of importance were held frequently the standard of information and understanding of many issues in the community would rise. But there are very severe limits on the capacity of everybody to be adequately informed about every thing that is of importance to them, given even the best will in the world, and we would need very much better channels of information than our present mass media. Moreover, the significance of one vote among millions is so small that it must seem pointless to most people to bother about most issues. When in doubt the devil you know is better than the devil you don't know. The result would almost certainly be a mass of very short-sightedly conservative decisions if most people voted on most issues. If, on the other hand, only those with some stake in the issue tended to vote in any particular referendum the result would be a large change of electorate from issue to issue, almost certainly resulting in inconsistent decisions. Inconsistent directives cannot be obeyed. They must be amended, at least in part.

The only way that is not dictatorial is negotiation. It is theoretically possible, of course, that such negotiations might be controlled by a series of iterated referendums, but the cost in time and effort and the exiguousness of the benefits even to the collectivity, let alone the individual, rule such a solution out in practice, at least in societies of the scale and complexity of ours. On most of the issues that affect us most of us have no strong opinions. We would like them to be decided by able, well-informed people with our interests at heart.

Voting in elections

The electoral system is supposed to fill this need. Very often the strongest single influence on the outcome of elections is not substantive issues as much as the candidate's or party's competence and performance.[6] The swinging voter is, by definition, not strongly committed on the outstanding issues between the major parties or coalitions. He or she often regards the choice between the parties on issues as a matter of emphasizing now one set of factors, now another, as circumstances change. But whether such emphases are effective in practice depends on the skill and responsiveness of the executive branch of government. Better a capable and reasonably responsive and responsible executive of a colour that is not to one's taste than a more congenial but incompetent or inflexible government. The question, then, is how well can voting perform when the task is seen not as the hopeless one of producing policy but its normal task of producing governments?

The usual way of choosing political representatives is by geographically based electorates each choosing one or more candidates to represent that electorate. There is no doubt that electoral systems are always very artificial contrivances which are sensitive to only a few of the factors that might reasonably be regarded as relevant.

Simple plurality voting with single-representative constituencies usually results in more conservative decisions than would result if minorities who are strongly dissatisfied with the status quo could express the strength of their preferences.[7] No doubt a certain amount of vote-trading does go on between interest groups through the brokerage of political parties. But the power of any group to make its desires count in that context is much more a matter of their having enough of what other groups want to trade for concessions than of the strength of their desires. It is true, of course, that not all people vote to secure some specific interest of their own. Many identify their own broad interests with the interests of just and sound administration. They are prepared to support groups that are manifestly disadvantaged and also to support platforms and candidates that promise to produce a reasonable balance between conflicting interests. But their perceptions and understanding of many of those interests is bound to be very incomplete and overlaid by conventional stereotypes. The benevolent concern of others is no substitute for power to make one's own needs count.

Another nest of difficulties is connected with the well-known problems of voter's order of preference among alternatives. I have only one vote on a certain question and there are three alternatives, and my first preference is rejected. Should I not then have a vote about which is to be preferred between the other two? Systems of preferential voting such as those used in Australia or of iterated voting such as is used in France, are attempts to deal with this problem. Again, in most systems of voting an interest group might constitute almost half of every constituency and not win in any. By contrast a group of similar aggregate numbers concentrated in a smaller number of constituencies might emerge as the most powerful group, winning every constituency in which it is present. It is notorious that there is no general solution to such difficulties. Any solution will tend to have very different outcomes, some of them highly undesirable, in different circumstances.

It is often possible to design a voting system that under the given circumstances will approach more nearly than any other to ensuring that major identified interest group can be represented roughly in proportion to its numbers. For such systems to be workable it is usually necessary that the number of interest groups to be represented be relatively small, cohesive over a wide range of issues and fairly clearly distinguishable from each other. Nevertheless, the representation can never be such that it is manifestly fair and guarantees that the emerging government will be fully representative. So most contemporary discussions insist that the problem to be solved is that of producing an unequivocal and reasonably satisfactory answer to the question, Who is to form the government in a nation-state?

The point of voting is not so much to represent the variety of interests of those who have a vote but to produce a decision that will be accepted by nearly everybody as final. This comes out most clearly in relatively small committees, where the vote is essentially a device for terminating discussion at a point where some suitable degree of consensus has been reached, or where it is impossible or unprofitable to prolong the discussion. The worth of the vote is almost wholly a function of the quality of the discussion and negotiation that have produced the alternatives that finally come to the vote.

In practice, in all modern electoral systems, that comes down to the soundness of political parties as a means of forming governments. Where the choice is between two parties each with a comprehensive and well-thought-out programme, there may be little to choose between them. The vote amounts to not much more than the toss of a coin. At the other extreme, when all the alternative governments are unacceptable there is little that votes can do to remedy the situation. So the worth of electoral democracy is closely bound up with the processes of party politics.

II ELECTORAL POLITICS

The function of elections is usually thought to be to produce a government, whether in a nation-state, a province or even a voluntary organization. The government is produced by competition among rival parties for the requisite number of votes of the electorate. Once elected a government is normally not subject to recall until the next election occurs. According to some it is very desirable that the elected government be free to pursue its policies, within the limits of the constitution, until it must face the electorate again. According to others the elected government should be constrained by as many organized pressure groups as are needed to make it responsive to the diverse needs in the community. However, even in the latter case the pressures that can be brought to bear on a government are usually effective in proportion to their bearing on elections to come.

The classical view, expressed by Mill, was that the electoral process should be so designed as to encourage voters to elect suitably qualified community representatives rather than agents for their specific interests. Such a view is, surprisingly, often reinforced by the development of highly disciplined parties. A great many people judge political parties not so much by their programmes as by their style of political action. Let us grant for the sake of argument that it is more important that the business of governing be well conducted than that some specific minority interests they favour be promoted at the cost of considerable failure in other areas. The problem is whether such assessments can in fact be made on a sound basis and given effect in the electoral process.

The process itself unfortunately tends to produce distorted results in quite systematic ways. Some of these are:

Mystifying issues

There has been much complaint and misgiving about the use of advertising techniques and image-making in electoral campaigns. But the mystification that matters most begins much further back. Overwhelming pressures to lie, to pretend, to conceal, to denigrate or sanctify are always present when the object to be sold is intangible and its properties unverifiable until long after the time when the decision to buy can be reversed. Sound strategy demands that in bidding for votes one pays out as little as possible in clear commitments and plays down any unpopular aspects of policies one is committed to. Usually it pays the opposition to concentrate more on spinning their own deceptive webs than on attempting to pin their opponents down. They fear being pinned down themselves. It is safer to stick to slogans and empty rhetoric, or to play on people's fear and prejudices. It pays to fight myth with myth.

Agglomeration of issues

The voters have no opportunity of separating issues out from each other. The result is that voters with a single dominant interest can be made to vote for a package of things they do not like in order to secure their major interest. Of course it is necessary and desirable that people have to make concessions to other interests in order to protect their own. The problem is that the packages are constructed, not with a view to getting the most acceptable compromise, but to achieving the one that suits the political strategy of the constructor.[8]

Professionalization of politics

The constructors of programmes and political images are increasingly professionals who organize and use power to advance their own careers. The progress of careers in an organization such as a party is determined mainly by the internal politics of the party. This would not matter, perhaps, if the processes of those politics resulted in coherent choices. But in the nature of the case they cannot generally do so. What concessions are made, and where, become a matter of contingencies that bear no systematic relation to the substantive problems. Some who have a weak case will be appeased because they are powerful or strategically placed. Others with stronger needs will be ignored or dismissed with mere rhetoric because they are not well organized or articulate. The needs of particular politicians to mobilize support determine which voices are recognized and which unheard.

These complaints are familiar enough. Because we are so familiar with them it is difficult to appreciate just how serious they are in practice. Clearly, in a stable and relatively homogeneous set of electorates they may not be thought to matter very much. In fact it may be argued that the interests of voters are more likely to be served by professional power-brokers than by committed people who act on principle. People may be better served by those who are looking for clients than by those who are looking for followers. It is not my task to adjudicate this debate. The crucial point is that neither alternative is satisfactory. The leaders will sacrifice their followers to their own visions and power-brokers will sacrifice weak clients to retain or gain strong ones. Both will attempt to narrow the choices open to their supporters, to prevent alternative leaders from emerging and to confront their followers or clients with an all-or-nothing choice.

In these circumstances it is very questionable whether elections can be regarded as anything more than a working arrangement for bringing about changes of government. Such changes are necessary from time to time if the political process is not to become too fixed in one mould. The defence of electoral democracy is reduced to the claim that it is preferable for this reason to other systems of government. Notoriously other systems of government, whatever their merits, usually fail at this task. To look upon elections as a means of choosing the best representatives is to expect too much of them. The performance of some candidates is known. The rest merely show some promise. There is little basis for most people to make a sound judgement. Again, when it comes to policies, the set of proposals that a party puts forward is usually in response to a situation that will have changed significantly by the time they can be implemented. One trouble with politicians is that they often break their promises. Another is that they often keep them, in spite of their no longer being appropriate.

Granted the impossibility of arriving at rationally aggregated preferences by any mechanical procedure and the desirability of negotiated settlements of conflicts that exploit the possibilities of the specific situation, it is probably desirable that governments not be precommitted to very specific proposals. This is particularly so if the proposals can be implemented from above only by increasing bureaucratic control, which is likely to be costly, often ineffectual and always difficult to direct and contain. Politics oscillates between efforts to use the government as a means of social change and disillusion with the results of such efforts and the costs they impose.

Negative control of government

The more important side of the process of political accommodation occurs not in the electoral process but in the process of government itself. To the extent that there is a large variety of organized interest groups that are free to combine or manoeuvre among themselves in response to government initiatives the power of government is restrained. Such groups can greatly increase the cost of initiatives they dislike by refusing to co-operate, by mobilizing the opposition of other groups and by playing on the fears of the public. The task of stopping a measure is very easy where there is no onus

of providing a positive alternative. A dozen conflicting interests may be united only in their opposition to a particular
proposal. If their aim is simply to stop the proposal their very
diversity of interests can be a source of strength. If each insists that only a proposal that meets all the interests of the
parties is acceptable, the line against the objectionable proposal can be held very easily, since the coalition cannot be
broken down. The costs of any member deserting are too
high. To betray all the other parties is to invite retaliation, or
at least strong distrust.

Increasingly the politics of lobbying those in power also
becomes professionalized. The profession of politics at every
level becomes one of power-broking and patronage.

The vast range of appointments to various offices that
governments have at their disposal are used to buy support
for those in power. Even those who are not just venal
careerists are forced to join in the scramble for position.
Without an institutionalized power base one has no leverage
within the system. Electoral politics merely reinforces this
tendency.

The primacy of power-broking

In order to be elected one has to attract votes. In order to
attract votes one has to be known and assessed. In most cases
people do not and cannot have adequate information to
assess a candidate's policies, ability or moral qualities. So
they rely on the verdict of a party that endorses candidates.
Such reliance is notoriously very weakly justified. Whatever
the various methods used by parties in selecting candidates, in
practice the decisions are made by a small number of people,
whether they be a central committee or the local branch activists or the party backers who support candidates in primary
elections. These groups almost always represent a quite narrow range of interests and make their choices on strategic or
tactical grounds rather than on the merits of the candidates.

The faithful party hack or loyal worker for the faction is preferred whenever it is possible to do so without risk of electoral failure, and sometimes even at the cost of failure at the polls.

The process of selection of candidates does very little to ensure that able legislators and administrators are selected, except perhaps for some of the most salient positions. It is, I think, fairly obvious that many of those who are elected to high office in most democratic countries are undistinguished in most relevant respects. The reason many abler and better people give for not going into politics is that they are not well equipped to deal with the continual jockeying for influence and position in party life, the toadying to those already in positions of power, the necessity of discrediting others rather than co-operating with them, the subordination of issues to tactics and so on. Of course, these features are not confined to political parties. They are characteristic of all organizations where there is competition for advancement and no firm, clear and independently sanctioned criteria of suitability for advancement. They affect parties in single-party and non-democratic regimes even more severely than democratic parties. Clearly elections impose limits on the degradation of selection criteria. Even hard-core party supporters will refuse to vote for some candidates.

Nevertheless, electoral politics does breed party politics, and party politics breeds mediocrity and corruption. Even where the local branch of a party is largely autonomous and formally democratic it is extremely easy for a cohesive group to gain control and manipulate rules and procedures to keep others out, unless they are even better organized and more determined. In practice such organization and motivation are usually found only among fringe or extreme groups who want to use the party as a means of advancing their interests rather than the ones for which it stands in the eyes of most voters. Such tactics may on occasions result in a rejuvenation of a party and of the political life of the nation. More often they degenerate into a sterile 'numbers game' which soon alienates from political life all those whose main interest is not power but substantive issues.

Parties choose the policies and teams of candidates that are put to electors, not on the basis of the needs or the wishes of the electors but on the basis of the relative power of various groups in the party and their specific interests as power-brokers. To be successful in politics one has to play this game and play it to win. There is no way of making parties much better than they are. A party is an organization designed to enforce a political line by exercising as much control as possible over its members. To gain electoral success it must confront the voters with a narrow choice between accepting the package it offers and an unacceptable alternative. To do so it must guard against splits at all costs. It must be strongly disciplined. Discipline is attained only by concentrating power to enforce decisions in relatively few hands, together with judgements about how to use that power. A party cannot rely entirely on self-discipline and co-operation among its members precisely because they are competing for power among themselves. There is little room for loyalty in power politics. The ruthless, the opportunists, those who are prepared to break their undertakings, very often win, and winners are rarely punished.

Inappropriate centralization and decentralization

Where party discipline is weak, power in many matters devolves on to local branches. The most frequent result is 'pork-barrelling'. The local politicians attempt to promote those issues and persons that combine a reasonable electoral appeal with the greatest possible advantage to those who control the local party branch. Electoral politics tend to decentralize power in matters where more central control is desirable and centralize power where decentralized control is desirable. Obviously this effect is difficult to prove and will be very variable according to a number of other factors. However, a number of important mechanisms are at work to produce the tendency, and there are few countervailing ones.

Let us look first at inappropriate decentralization. The most obvious factor here is local chauvinism. It is always relatively easy to mobilize local support for a policy that brings tangible benefits to a local community or enables it to hold on to advantages it possesses, no matter what the effects of its doing so may be on outsiders. It is almost inevitable that chauvinistic issues will be much more strongly supported and less divisive than broader issues. So there will be a strong 'democratic' pull to make the electoral system sensitive to them. On the other hand, issues that concern a more generalized devolution of power have no special appeal to any one local electorate. The more general issues are perceived as remote and less important.

Where decentralization simply means centralization on a smaller scale, bringing as many issues and powers as possible together under a single local authority, it is of very dubious value. The agglomeration of issues is, if anything, more pernicious at the local level than at the level of the nation state. At the local level it is much easier for the formal legal and institutional means of control and the informal power structures of the community to be knit together so closely as to suppress any effective challenge to them. Almost all issues come to be considered primarily in relation to the problem of preserving the cohesiveness and power of the local community. In practice, of course, that usually means the power of a small group within that community. But even if power is not highly concentrated within a local community, there are very narrow limits to the amount of variation that it can allow while still maintaining itself as a total community, an appropriate locus for centralizing almost all decision-making. It must resist changes that make for stronger links between members of the community and outsiders. It must deny the validity of claims that outsiders make upon it.

To sum up, decentralized democratic control by electoral processes is likely to produce a static and oppressive local chauvinism of a very conservative kind, the mirror, in fact, of the worst aspects of nationalism. I am arguing throughout that an appropriate form of decentralization would concentrate on functions rather than localities. The organizations that supply various community needs should be independent of each other. Their geographical extent should vary according to the technical and social exigencies of their carrying out those functions. Such a great diversity of authorities with different circumscriptions could not be managed by electoral processes, as we shall see. But that is no disadvantage.

That electoral control leads to inappropriate centralization is less controversial. As we saw in discussing bureaucracy, it is often the case that higher layers of bureaucratic control have no other defensible function than to bring a number of functional units under central control, not in the interests of efficiency but simply for the sake of control. Electoral politics involves putting the responsibility for the production of common goods in the hands of unitary central authorities. These authorities must find means of controlling the agencies for which they are responsible. Control has to be centralized irrespective of efficiency or flexibility. Putting each of these various agencies under its own popularly elected board would not solve the problem. In practice most electors could know very little about the candidates and the issues in the host of institutions by which they are affected. In most cases they would have to vote for party tickets, which is really a way of returning these bodies to centralized control.

Voting systems

A great deal has been written about the properties of various systems of voting, especially plurality, majority and proportional systems. A fully adequate dismissal of electoral democracy would have to show that none of these systems can remedy the defects we have discussed. There have been numerous discussions of the relative merits of the various methods of computing votes both from highly theoretical and very practical points of view. But these discussions normally assume that the problem is that of providing a government for a nation-state, which is just the assumption that is under attack in this book.

Very roughly, plurality and majority systems tend to produce two large parties or stable coalitions that in most circumstances compete for the middle ground and offer alternative administrations which differ only in emphasis. It is possible, however, especially in a plurality system, for the parties to diverge, each pursuing a fairly extreme policy and hoping that the middle ground will be more afraid of their opponents' extremism than of theirs. Proportional representation seems to offer less possibility of government being dominated either by the middle or by an extreme of the political spectrum. In fact, however, proportional representation does not ensure a multiplicity of parties corresponding to the various hues of the spectrum. In many countries it works in what is virtually a two-party manner, sometimes to bring those parties into convergence, sometimes into confrontation. Even when it does result in a multiplicity of parties these tend to have more destructive than constructive power. It is much easier to immobilize the governmental machine than to set it going in a specific direction. The fact is that there is no voting system that cannot be manipulated by a large, well-organized and well-placed political party to ensure that it gets a great deal more of the power than its proportion of the vote would warrant.

In effect, the achievement of electoral systems is that they make it possible peacefully to eject a government and replace it with a government that is at least less disagreeable to the largest cohesive group of voters. But this gain is a gain only when compared with other systems of tenure of office that rest on heredity or co-option or military force. It probably has few disadvantages that are not shared by those other systems, but equally it shares most of their disadvantages. It inspires the loyalty that it has won mainly because the known alternatives are so repulsive. We can do better.

III THE ALTERNATIVE TO ELECTORAL DEMOCRACY

Negotiation and size

I have already argued that most issues of any complexity need to be settled by negotiation in a co-operative framework. The most advantageous feasible solution for each party is often possible only if it is prepared to make concessions to other parties who are in a position to block many of the possible outcomes. In any case there are almost always long-term advantages in encouraging reciprocity by striving to achieve solutions that are at least seen as fair by all involved. Negotiation involves attempts to construct comprehensive packages through a process of exploration of possibilities, expanding or contracting the scope of the packages, trying to get clear about what is important and what is negotiable for each party.

Such work must be done in committee. The point of the small committee, the reason why large assemblies often refer problems to them, is that the members of the committee can spare the time to familiarize themselves with all the details of a matter in a way that is not possible to most members of the assembly, granted the range of other problems demanding their attention. Moreover, in informal debate in a committee, the members can explore and construct a wide variety of possible solutions to a problem and attempt to find ways of conciliating divergent interests. The larger assembly, by contrast, is usually capable only of accepting or rejecting a given proposal, perhaps with some minor amendments.

Committees, precisely because they cannot claim to be fully representative of all the interests involved may come under strong pressure to demonstrate that they have made every effort to take them all into account. Committees strive to achieve as much unanimity as possible in their final proposals because unanimity enhances the force of their decision. Committees tend to accommodation, large assemblies to confrontation. In the large assembly there is neither the time not the capacity for detailed negotiation, and partly because of this each agent is usually reduced to representing a single interest. Each member of a large body can have some impact on the outcome only by making some single clear and telling point. By and large in such situations it is easier to be effective in stopping proposals than in proposing constructive alternatives.

The large assembly is usually forced to bring the question to a vote whether or not it has been discussed adequately. In modern parliamentary situations party discipline ensures that government sponsored legislation goes through with the minimum of amendment. The committees in which the real work of negotiation is done conduct their meetings in secret, sometimes because they are in fact clandestine, sometimes behind a veil of officially sanctioned 'confidentiality'. Clearly it is desirable that negotiations on public policy decisions should be conducted publicly. At the same time, however, the negotiators should be free to consider alternatives without being called to heel by those whose interests they represent. The process of exploration of possibilities cannot proceed if pressure groups are in a position to lay down in advance what is negotiable and what is not.

Representation and function

Two main reasons why one ought to entrust the furtherance of one's interests to somebody else are the opportunity costs of pursuing them oneself and one's lack of the appropriate knowledge and skill. My representative should have at least as strong an interest in advancing my interests as I have, should be in a position to devote more time and effort to the task and bring to it superior knowledge and skill. It is very unlikely that anybody can meet these requirements in regard to my interests generally, or even my interest in public goods. But once one specifies a particular interest, the local library, for example, it is quite likely that there are people who share my interests, have a stronger motivation to work for them than I do, and are better equipped to do so.

If the range of interests that I have, many of them con-flicting interests, are to be properly represented, it is most unlikely that any one person will be appropriate.[9] What I need is a host of specialized representatives each of whom has the same interest as I in the relevant respect, and the appro-priate motivation, knowledge and skill. How is it possible for me to have such representation?

In most democratic countries a large number of common goods are provided at local level by municipal councils, which are elected by the residents (or property-holders) in a certain area and draw the bulk of their revenue from taxes, especially on landed property, that they levy on residents or property-holders in that area. Among the functions of these bodies the salient ones are usually to lay down and enforce rules about and provide services in areas such as town planning and building regulations, public health, garbage disposal, parks and recreational facilities, local roads and drainage, libraries and some educational facilities, environmental protection and the promotion of local industry. The basic reasons why these different functions are vested in the same body are: (1) that it is the source of finance for them, and (2) that it is the means by which the exercise of those functions is controlled in some degree by the governed. There is no particularly strong rela-tion between the functions themselves. Many of them have stronger practical links with similar functions in neighbouring municipalities or in higher levels of government than with other functions at the local level. It is not always the case that the geographical area of a municipality is the most suitable unit from the point of view of efficiency of operations. It is not very likely that a library authority and a garbage disposal authority for example would break up into the same geographical units, particularly in the large conurbations in which most people in Western countries now live. The city, the town, the suburb no longer exist as communities in the way that they did when the structure of our patterns of local government was formed. People's activities take place in a variety of localities and they belong to many overlapping communities, most of which have no precise location or boundaries or membership.

Of the two reasons given above why these various functions are united in the same body, the first, that it provides the bulk of the finance for them is historically important but not very cogent, since there is no particular reason why each of these functions should draw its revenue from the same source. Even if they did, the function of the fundraising body might simply be that of apportioning funds to a variety of agencies, leaving the responsibilities for deciding on what use is to be made of those funds to the agencies themselves, provided there is appropriate control of those agencies by some other means. So the decisive reason for making a single body responsible for a variety of functions is that it is a way of keeping some degree of democratic control over their operations. What this form of organization does is to add an administrative level to the levels that are required to perform the specific functions and attempt to achieve democratic control of all of them through this level. The obvious alternative would be to have specific elections for the controlling bodies in each function. The advantages would be numerous. Representatives with particular interest in one or other of the bodies would nominate for it. The number of opportunities for people to take an active role in public life would be increased enormously, and many people who would not be willing to set themselves the whole range of problems of a municipal council would probably be willing to take a strong interest in a particular function, especially if in doing so they had a fairly free hand.

The central difficulty, of course, is that there would be too many elections. Each voter would belong to many different electorates, and most would lack the time, information and motivation to make any informed personal judgement about most of them. In practice most people, if they bothered to vote, would tend to vote for party lists or 'tickets'. The net result might well be simply to strengthen the party apparatuses. The game of power-trading and building a power base would tend to take precedence over the specific issues involved. The value of functional representation would be lost.

Representation and sampling

The most reliable way of getting a group that is representative of a particular population is to take a statistical sample of the population. The theory and practice of sampling is now highly developed. Such a representative group could be trusted to act as representatives if they had some stronger than average motive for devoting themselves to the interests they represent and acquiring adequate knowledge and skill for the task. If they were compensated for the time and effort involved the mere fact of their being chosen to be representatives might be sufficient motivation for many. For others it would, like jury service today, be an unwelcome imposition.

It seems preferable, therefore, that representatives should be volunteers. Once a statistical characterization of the various interests to be represented is established there should be no problem in selecting from those who are willing to serve a group that is representative in the statistical sense.[10] Granted that they volunteer to work in this particular area rather than some other or none, it is likely that they feel more strongly than most people about the issues involved and that they have or are prepared to acquire superior knowledge of the problems. So it would be reasonable for the group that these people represent statistically to accept them as representatives in decision-making. One could envisage a well-based convention granting authority to such bodies and appropriate procedures for selecting them.

The first thing that would need to be clearly defined is the function to be supervised and a reasonably comprehensive analysis of the various interests that people might have in the supervision of that function. In general the main groups affected would be those who work at providing the good in question, those who are consumers of it and those who are affected by its side-effects. But within these groups there might well be very substantial conflicts of interest and differences of opinion.

So the question immediately arises whether it is interest or opinions that are to form the basis of selection. There is no insuperable difficulty in either case. One could take a broad opinion survey, classify groups of opinions and choose representatives on the basis of their own answers to the survey questions so as to match the strength of the various opinions in the population. There would be some incentive for those with unpopular opinions to disguise them in the hope of being chosen. It is statistically unlikely, however, that this would affect the result substantially unless a very large proportion of those who volunteer to serve entered into a conspiracy to manipulate the sampling process. There could be safeguards against this possibility. Candidates might be required to declare publicly their beliefs and the interests they claim to represent and even be liable to legal actions for gross misrepresentation or fraud.

Such a system would still leave representatives a great deal of room for negotiation, and even for changing their opinions whenever they had defensible ground for doing so. It would approximate more closely than any other system to a fully participatory democracy. The main objection to it is that if people are not very well informed about a matter and express opinions about it in relative isolation those opinions are not well-grounded. There is no good reason for taking them seriously as the basis for structuring the body that is to make the decisions.

The objection could be met by making the survey not a matter of 'off the cuff' answers to a questionnaire but an educative and exploratory exercise. A demographically representative sample could be chosen and the people in the sample could be given special information and opportunities for discussions about the issues before giving their answers. Perhaps they might even be paid to take the time to study the problems. Such measures might be expected to improve the quality of the basis for choosing representatives, the quality of the representatives and the general quality of on-going debate in the community about such matters. They would not abolish conflicts of interest or differences of opinion, but they would create an atmosphere of rational open and constructive discussion in which optimal solutions would be most likely to emerge and gain acceptance.

In most situations, however, such an elaborate method of choosing representatives might not be warranted. It would be simpler to choose them on the basis of an analysis of the interests involved. Interests are more important and even more cogent in the long-run than opinions. Rationally I should prefer my interests to be safeguarded rather than have my more or less shaky opinions prevail. In practice, of course, I may often set a higher priority on getting my own way than on securing my long-term interests because of pride, spite, impatience, stupidity or other human failings. But most of us in most matters that affect us do not have such a definite will. Even when we know what we would like to happen we are well aware that if we knew all the relevant facts our practical choice could well be different.

Moreover, in many cases there is no 'right' decision. Our long-term interests are not fixed. Different and largely incommensurable possibilities exist. Choosing one or other of those possibilities means entering a different situation in which some of our tastes, hopes and relationships will change. There is no unchanging point of reference, no fixed set of needs or preferences, against which such possibilities can be so measured and evaluated as to produce a right answer. There are indeed many wrong answers. It is not the case that we are infinitely malleable. We need to be assured that clearly wrong choices are not made. But the quest for a way of finding *the* right answer is radically pointless.

In general it is more in our interests that a variety of possibilities be explored than that attempts should be made to discover and impose what purports to be the best way of dealing with a problem. The great strength of the case for the superiority of the market over planning is just such a point. However, allowing great opportunities for diverse solutions to problems, diverse projections of needs, and differing opinions to be tried is not an exclusive property of the market. If representatives in charge of various functional enterprises had a free hand to try whatever solutions they thought best there is little doubt that a great variety of ways of doing things would be tried. I shall argue that this would be an advantage and that it need not carry with it any serious disadvantages.

Representation and responsibility

In some circumstances we may sensibly consent to be represented by a person over whom we have no control. In some circumstances we may reasonably be presumed to consent to being represented by somebody without even knowing what is going on. But the relationship of representation is undoubtedly stronger in proportion to the degree of willingness of the person represented to accept the representative. In political contexts it has commonly been assumed that the degree in which a polity is democratic is proportional to the degree of control that the citizens have over their representatives. Clearly acceptance is not enough or any legitimate regime would be democratic. Some authoritarian regimes may have enjoyed as high a degree of acceptance as many a democracy.

What control involves is not as simple as it might at first seem. If one is in a position to decide quite determinately what one wants the degree of control one has over a representative is just a matter of one's capacity to ensure that the representative acts as effectively as possible to implement one's decision. Corporate bodies, especially large bodies of people with diverse interests in relation to a type of activity, are not in a position to have a fully determinate will about the practical matters to be decided. They may, of course, have many areas of agreement and share a number of aspirations, but a host of issues remain to be resolved. There is in general no correct resolution of these issues and no correct procedure of arriving at a resolution of them. In other words, there cannot be anything like Rousseau's *general will*, as he himself recognized, except in the very simplest societies. There can only be conventions to accept certain results or decision procedures for the sake of getting things done, So, for example, there is no right system of voting. As long as the results are not too disastrous we agree to abide by the results of the system we have simply because it is accepted. It is the convention.

But do we, in order to have democracy, have to find a way in which the *demos* first makes up its mind what is to be done and then controls its representatives in the process of carrying it out? What I want to suggest is a different conception. Let the convention for deciding what is our common will be that we will accept the decision of a group of people who are well informed about the question, well-motivated to find as good a solution as possible and representative of our range of interests simply because they are statistically representative of us as a group. If this group is then responsible for carrying out what it decides, the problem of control of the *execution* process largely vanishes. Those directing the execution process are carrying out their own decisions. They may need a little prodding to keep them up to the mark, but there is no institutional basis for a conflict of interest between bodies responsible for making decisions and those responsible for execution. They have an overriding interest in showing that their decisions were practical and well-grounded.

Granted that this process may be expected to generate effective social decisions and actions the question comes down to the sense in which the people control the decision-making process. It is useful to look at this question first statistically and then in terms of the dynamics of representation. If the group making a decision is statistically representative of the group on whose behalf it is made then it is very likely that the decision will be in accord with the result of some reasonable decision procedure for that group. The statistical selection procedure controls the distribution of the interests represented and so controls the decisions that are likely to emerge by rational negotiations among those representatives. Granted a sound statistical procedure the people automatically control the broad outlines of the result simply by being what they are. The mapping ensures a correspondence between the character of the representatives and the represented. Again, the group of representatives are all themselves members of the people. Nobody is selected because of professional knowledge or skill or prestige or privilege or institutional position. What the representatives are expected to bring to the decision process is that sensitivity to the interests involved that comes from having those interests. They are supposed to be typical of those affected by the decisions to be made. The decisions that the representatives will arrive at will differ from the actual wishes of those they represent because better information and the results of negotiations will make a difference. However, this is precisely the divergence from one's actual views that a rational person is normally willing to accept in the actions of a delegate.

Naturally, the mere fact that representatives come from a certain social group does not guarantee that they will cherish the interests of that group. They may be quite deluded about what those interests are. They may put some other interest they have ahead of the interests they are supposed to represent. They may be bribed or bought off. What safeguards are there against these things? One safeguard against delinquency is to suppress the causes that tend to produce temptations. Most of these fall within a wider context of property arrangements and social rewards that we shall look at later on. The crucial question, however, is that of public scrutiny. Everything that these committees do must be open to inspection. It is not difficult to ensure this if there are enough people around who follow closely what is done and have a strong motivation for making public anything that others would like to conceal.

If political office is attained by lot there are no professional political careers. Nobody has to acquire debts to party organizations or patrons in order to gain office or to hang on to it. The usual pressures to keep quiet are absent. On the other hand, the greatest reward that a person is likely to get from public service is recognition of his or her ability and integrity. In any committee, granted that there will be a diversity of interests and loyalties there are almost certainly going to be people who will expose any attempts to suborn members of the committee. Moreover, since membership would change in a regular pattern there would rapidly grow up a body of experienced, informed people who would have an interest in the doings of their successors and try to expose their errors or delinquencies, if only to enhance their own record.

More positively, it seems very likely that high standards of presentation of proposals for public discussion and responsiveness to the results of such discussion would emerge. Since the representatives would not be up for re-election they could afford to look at the various objections and suggestions raised on their merits. In some cases they might do things that were quite unpopular with a majority in the interests of a disadvantaged minority. In others they might assert a majority interest in spite of the objections of a powerful minority. The cheap rhetoric of political discourse would lose in representative committees. Ultimately their motivation would be to be recognized as having done a good job. Whether or not to be held in high regard is the strongest of motivations for people generally, there can be little doubt that it is always a strong motivation for the sort of people who are attracted to public office.

In a large and complex society very few people can be well known to the general public. Very many people, however, can be well known in some specialized activity. If that activity becomes the focus for a partial community, fame within it can be a significant reward, especially if the activity is in turn seen as important to the wider community or complex of partial communities.

Representation and co-ordination

It is not too difficult to envisage the solution I have proposed to the problem of democratic control of functional units producing specific public goods and services. The problems of co-ordination between these units are in many respects much easier than is often imagined. For the most part they can be left to negotiation between the bodies concerned, once the obstacles that bureaucratic structures place in the way of co-operation are removed. To a large extent the common good consists in the good functioning of a number of services that conjointly meet our various needs. The substantive criteria of good functioning are derived not from some higher-order set of concepts but from the specific tasks and the social realities in which they are embedded.

The point of democracy is to govern society from within the specific groupings that constitute the relevant population for each of the different public activities. The whole grows by the growth of the parts. The whole is integrated by each part adjusting itself continuously to the others with which it interacts. The illusion that democracy can be assured by so-called democratic control of the state is disastrous. The state cannot be controlled democratically. It must be abolished.

Of course, it is desirable that general movements of social thought and aspiration in the community should find expression in the overall direction of public policy. There is no reason, however, why these emphases and preferences should not be developed through their influence on the decisions of the representatives who share them. In this way they are likely to find more appropriate, diverse and direct expression than if that expression were mediated by electoral and bureaucratic processes. The spirit of public policy should in these circumstances reflect the spirit of the most articulate and responsible members of the community.

Higher-level bodies

Nevertheless there remain important problems in setting up the various functional bodies, hearing appeals about their structure, restructuring them to meet changed circumstances, adjudicating their disagreements and dividing up resources between them. Determining these matters would be the task of higher-order bodies which would seek to adjudicate conflicting claims in the light of generally accepted criteria. Such bodies, on the view I am advocating, would not be empowered to initiate policy, much less to dictate to various functional bodies, but to provide a legal framework within which productive bodies operate. There are important questions about how such bodies are to be prevented from exceeding their legal role and becoming administrative authorities. For the moment, however, I am concerned about the sense in which they ought to be representative.

Very roughly, what I want to argue is that it would be appropriate for them to be representative neither of interest nor opinions but of the social experience of the community. The people chosen to staff such bodies should have substantial firsthand experience of the problems and practices of first-order functional bodies. They should be able and trusted. The best way to meet these requirements would be to choose them by lot from a pool of candidates nominated by their colleagues on first-order bodies as having shown the special skill, knowledge and dedication that would fit them for a judicial role. They would constitute a sample of those judged most suited to the task by those in the best position to know.[11]

In their decision-making such bodies would work by a case-based rather than rule-based procedure, arguing by analogy for the relevance of various considerations and moderating precedent in the light of new circumstances. Since they, too, would have only a limited term of office, there would be plenty of opportunity for variation within a reasonable continuity. No professional class would emerge but a body of interested, informed critics would be formed who would be at liberty to criticize judgements. There would not be any need, I believe, for protection of these legal processes by the permanent threat of sanctions. I assume that responsible public functional bodies would not be nearly as likely as private citizens or corporations to reject a reasonably constituted judicial body's authority. In most cases they would be brought to heel by sanctions from other bodies if they did.

In extreme cases, however, it might be possible to defy such judgements with impunity. Their being open to this threat would, I believe, operate as salutary restraint on any tendency of judicial bodies to step beyond their proper role. The society would cohere only as long as the conventions on which it was based were respected. Ultimately, of course, that is almost trivially true of any society. However, in a society where there is a centralized and overwhelmingly powerful police and military force, control of a sort can be maintained as long as the conventions that ensure control over that force hold. In the society I am envisaging the cohesion of the whole is dependent on a much more dispersed and varied set of conventions holding, simply because of the variety of social pressures that tend to maintain them.

Anarchy and community

In *Community, Anarchy and Liberty* Michael Taylor argued that anarchy in the strict sense, a social order without a state apparatus, is possible only if there is community. The three 'core characteristics' of community in Taylor's sense are: (1) The set of persons who compose a community have beliefs and values in common; (2) Relations between members should be direct and many sided; (3) There should be a high level of reciprocity, covering such things as exchanges, mutual aid, co-operation and sharing, as well as mutual enforcement of these arrangements.[12]

What I am suggesting, in effect, is that we can envisage a community of organizations rather than a community of individuals as constituting a modern society. It seems to me very doubtful whether the variety and capacity for change that are characteristic of modern mass technologically advanced societies can be preserved in small communities based on individuals. In modern societies individuals belong to a multiplicity of partial communities and organizations that are continually changing. Within various specific contexts they may have relations with other individuals that are communal, but their relations with the society as a whole are much more formal, legal, inflexible and impersonal. Taylor and many other anarchists want to restore small, face-to-face, relatively comprehensive communities. I am very doubtful whether this is either possible or desirable, though I cannot argue the matter in any detail here. The point I am trying to make is, in any case, independent of the possibility or desirability of community among individuals under modern conditions. Rather it is that there can, even on the modern scale, be community among certain kinds of organizations and partial communities, without their being a total community at any level.

Obviously a set of organizations devoted to producing a variety of public goods governed by representative members of the communities affected is likely to have many shared values and beliefs, particularly values and beliefs concerning the standards and procedures by which the organizations should operate. They will deal directly with each other and since each is highly specialized it will in practice have relations of interdependence with a number of other bodies. Finally, the pattern of exchanges between these bodies will be a matter of mutual trust and co-operation backed by sanctions of withdrawal of co-operation. The individual men and women responsible for carrying out the various functions that constitute these organizations would find themselves constrained to act in accordance with a communal pattern. Everything in their social relations, all the pressures on them, would conspire to make them conform to their roles.

Although that would not necessarily produce an atmosphere of community among those agents in matters outside their roles, it might well do so. It would be possible, pleasant and usually advantageous that there be an atmosphere of politeness, kindness, consideration, respect and friendliness among people. Such an atmosphere sustains a great deal of communal life even between strangers. It may not be strong enough to ensure the enforcement of social order. For that you need the tighter controls of the small community, as Taylor argues. But granted that the substance of social order is guaranteed on a non-repressive and co-operative basis a generalized sense of social co-operation can flourish fairly easily. In turn, such an atmosphere makes the task of ensuring social order very much less difficult in the residual areas where there are temptations to crime.

In other words, a sense of community, interdependence and reciprocity is not restricted to small communities or to relatively self-contained communities. If there is a sufficiently strong sense, diffused through a network of partial but overlapping communities, that doing favours for strangers one will never meet again, acting considerately towards everybody or being open to other people's points of view is itself pleasant and likely to be reciprocated, then the conduct of public affairs on a basis of reciprocity will appear natural. The principal condition for achieving such an atmosphere is to eliminate zero-sum conflicts from the structures of personal and social relationships as far as possible. In that way co-operative behaviour can become more than a veneer of morality and courtesy imposed on relations that constantly tend to confrontation. The ways in which entitlements to resources and rewards are generated and appropriated are crucial in this respect.

Protection of person and property

In a society in which people are free to change their jobs, their residence, their friends and their activities very easily, it is not difficult to kill, steal of injure without it being known who committed the crime. If it is known only in a small group it is easy to evade the sanctions that group can bring to bear. It is to be expected that many people will have strong motives for crime, and need to be deterred. In a complex and large society there seems no substitute for police forces. It is by no means clear, however, that there needs to be a single agency with global power to enforce the law in all areas, much less that such an agency should be the custodian of public morals. From the point of view of detention and investigation there can be a number of specialized agencies, as there are in effect within modern police forces. These agencies could co-operate rather than be under a single control.

The type of policing that seems to require an open brief is that of 'the cop on the beat', whose presence is supposed to deter criminals and ensure public order. That role went out with the motor car and the changes in the pattern of urban living. In any case, it was in its heyday primarily a means of controlling the poor, and especially the young, preventing the emergence of street gangs and the like. In so far as these or analogous functions remain in contemporary societies, there are better ways of dealing with them by provision of specific services and opportunities for those who have nothing better to do than fight or 'disturb the peace'.

Once again, the point is that a local authority is likely to be too total and too repressive, a wider-based authority too powerful and too subject to corruption. Specific law enforcement agencies dealing with specific kinds of problems are much more likely to be effective provided the problems of controlling them can be dealt with, and the structure can be changed to meet changing circumstances. Once these problems are clearly distinguished, they can be met at different levels by different kinds of bodies. The problems of supervision of specialized agencies can be handled by representative committees with managerial and policy-making powers. The problems of restructuring must be dealt with in a way that avoids giving to the body that decides on restructuring proposals any overall executive power. In no area is it more important to avoid centralization of power. The decisions must take the form of arbitration between conflicting proposals to extend the jurisdiction of existing agencies or create new agencies. The arbitrating body must have no power to engage in police work of any kind. It must not direct the policy of bodies that do so except by way of settlement of disputes.

It seems likely that, given reasonably active organs of public opinion, there would be little difficulty in holding higher-order bodies to their adjudicative role. The lower-order bodies would be jealous of their autonomy, and to some extent jealous of each other. It is not quite so clear, however, that in some other contexts, such as police work, a particular agency might not come to occupy such a strategic position in the complex of agencies that it would effectively dictate to the rest in crucial matters. It could be, for example, that an agency set up to guard against computer crime might, in a highly computerized society, gain the power to control any information transaction and thus any formal social action in that society. Its operations, moreover, might be extremely difficult to monitor, and virtually impossible for a lay person to understand.

There is no doubt that this kind of development would be controlled only by constant vigilance by people involved in the ordinary running of the dangerous agency.[13] These people would need to be given every incentive to keep the operations of the agency fully public, to discuss their problems and dangers and make proposals for change. There is, of course, an inherent tension between the need for a certain amount of guile in criminal investigation and the need for public accountability of the investigation. But the major deterrent to crime must always be the difficulty of concealing it in the first place. Publicity about the kinds of actions being taken to prevent crime is a sound deterrent if the actions are well conceived. If they are not well conceived the criminals are likely to be aware of it before the public in any case. Public scrutiny may detect problems if there is adequate discussion and it is certainly likely to encourage critical thinking within agencies. Such publicity about policy is quite compatible with discretion within the context of particular investigations.

In the day-to-day running of police agencies, as with other agencies, a balance will have to be struck between reasonable autonomy for the full-time professionals and adequate access to information for the lay supervisory bodies. There is no recipe for such a balance, and it cannot be denied that statistically representative bodies may from time to time be dominated by people who are so intrusive that they make sound professional work impossible, or so complacent that they do not exercise proper supervision. Nevertheless, compared to the present arrangements in most countries, it is hard to believe that such citizen committees would not on the whole constitute an enormous improvement. The links that at present exist between the people who control policing and the rest of the government powers, both constitutionally and informally through the party system, constitute a standing invitation to the abuse of police power for oppressive ends.

4

Democracy and markets

I PUBLIC AND PRIVATE GOODS AND EVILS

Goods, evils and control

Some goods are such that one person using them excludes anybody else from using them. They are, to that extent, private, in
the sense of benefiting only one person. If they are consumed
by a single use, like a piece of cake, they are necessarily
private. At the other end of the spectrum, some goods, like
lighthouses, are necessarily public, equally available to everybody. But many goods can be provided in either private or
public forms. It is a fairly tenacious characteristic of our
civilization that we tend to prefer as many things as possible to
be available to us in the form of private goods, even when there
is no technical necessity. We prefer private cars to public
transportation, private to communal facilities in our housing
and so on, even when it would be cheaper to rely on common
provision of such goods. It is a natural result of and condition of a flourishing market economy that we should. The
stimulus to compete lies in the advantage that is gained through
the possession of private goods. If the best things in life are
free, why work?

Nevertheless, many of the best things in life are largely free
– sunshine and wind and rain, language and the treasures it
contains, the beauty of people and streets, and many kinds of

knowledge. Not one of these is diminished by being used, much less destroyed. The shared enjoyment of them itself constitutes a good that is highly prized, as when our enjoyment of a play is enhanced by being part of a large and attentive audience. Moreover, there is a public aspect to most private goods, the landscape of houses and farms, the dress and comportment of people in public, the rhythm of life. In a healthy community many people contribute to the upkeep of such public goods because they prize them and enjoy contributing to them as well as receiving recognition for doing so. Why not make as much of life like that as possible? Why not supply as much of what we want as is possible in the form of public goods? People will work if they receive due recognition as public benefactors.

Before looking at these questions it is useful to look at bads and evils. The worst things in life are also 'free' in the sense that they very often come to people quite independently of their having done anything to produce or attract them. Evils are not just the lack of some needed good. They are positive things like war, threats to our livelihood, epidemic disease and an atmosphere of distrust or hatred. Whatever one's views about maximizing public goods there can be little question that an important task for any community is to protect itself against public evils. What is more controversial is whether people ought also to be protected against private evils. For our present purpose, however, what is important is that there is a significant difference between producing goods and producing evils. There is, with a few ominous exceptions, no market for evils, only a market for the means of combating them. They appear in the market as 'externalities'. The standard way of controlling them is by prohibition and penalty rather than by incentives not to produce them. To demand a price for not producing evils is extortion.[1]

The difficulty in controlling evils by prohibitions is that evils can easily be brought about by people doing what they are normally entitled to do. Merchants raise the price of grain, drive down the price of what people have to sell in exchange, and the result is famine, followed by epidemic disease and enormous social disruption and suffering. Famines, as Sen has shown,[2] have usually arisen not from an absolute shortage of grain but from a collapse of people's entitlements to buy it. They have nothing to sell that the market wants at that time at a price that is sufficient to cover their costs of survival. The market is an admirable mechanism for exchanging commodities between people with roughly comparable entitlements in situations where there is genuine choice available to both buyers and sellers. It can and does become the means whereby whole classes of people are deprived of effective choice when they must sell their whole energies to a few buyers at a minimal price, or where there are no buyers at all.

Not so long ago advocates of maximal market control of allocation of resources denied that these problems were serious any longer in the advanced industrial countries. But radically unacceptable patterns of distribution are, in fact, endemic in the market system. There is an inherent tendency for market success to generate concentration of ownership of resources and the power that that brings. There is a constant tendency for jobs to be destroyed by new technology, and the market cannot create new ones fast enough to avert great and undeserved misery in many cases. Clearly, where unacceptable results are the product of normal legitimate procedures, those results cannot be averted simply by prohibitions. There must be positive means of producing and allocating assistance to those in need and counteracting the unwanted consequences of market forces.

When the evils of unmitigated market control and the evils of bureaucracy are set against each other, the natural question to ask is whether or not there is some way in which the defects of each can be mitigated by the virtues of the other. So we have bureaucratic organizations designed to stabilize markets, control the concentration of capital, protect national interests in investment and employment and provide some 'social security'. On the other hand, the bureaucracy is controlled by the constant comparison of its efficiency with that of 'free enterprise', by resistance to the taxation needed to finance it, and by the general requirement that it not endanger the profitability of investment. This kind of compromise is inherently unstable and under constant attack from both 'socialist' and 'free market' advocates. So we are led to raise the question whether there is not some way of establishing, on the basis of objective principles, what sort of goods are appropriately produced and distributed by market mechanisms and what by other procedures.

Knowledge, for example, is not only not diminished but normally enhanced and made more fruitful by being shared as widely as possible in a community of knowledge. For a community of knowledge is constituted by people with appropriate critical skills, cognitive interests and means of developing knowledge. A piece of knowledge that is absorbed into such a community is critically evaluated, related to a variety of other relevant knowledge and developed in new ways. Similar considerations apply to the arts and their products. It is inherently undesirable that either the means of producing these things or their products should be sequestered and made the exclusive possession of any individual or group.

The trouble is that neither the means of producing cognitive and aesthetic products nor the products themselves exist in a purely spiritual form. They have material components and conditions. Their material embodiments, books, pictures, scores, instruments and so on, can be bought and sold. The labour, the facilities and the materials involved in the quest for and communication of knowledge and other mental goods have to be paid for. The community can foot the bill. But resources are not unlimited. So there have to be ways of providing those resources, for example by taxation, and apportioning them to those who are likely to use them to best effect. If these matters are handled bureaucratically they are likely to be mishandled and given a strongly conservative bias. Rules, precedents and routine procedures are not conducive to innovatory, critical and excellent work.

So perhaps there is a case for making cognitive goods into commodities as far as possible and leaving the provision of their material prerequisites to be met by the sale of such things as copyrights, courses and entry to exhibitions and shows. Apart from questions of general utility, the effects of such a practice are clearly unsatisfactory. It works very well for pop music, films and some fiction. It does not and cannot work at all for highly abstract knowledge such as physical theory of for the more difficult works of art.[3]

The provisional moral to be drawn from these considerations is that abstract considerations in these matters are extremely inconclusive. Even when a good seems at a certain level of abstraction to be completely public, it inevitably has aspects that are private when considered more concretely. Again it is possible to change a given material or spiritual thing from a mainly public good into a mainly private good by suitable social arrangements such as specified property rights. Finally, these changes have effects not only on how much of these goods are produced and who gets to use them or profit by their production. They even affect what is seen as good (or bad) about them, for example whether cultural achievements are seen as primarily collective achievements or as primarily the product of the individuals most closely identified with the final stage of their production.

What ought to be up for sale?

We need to look case by case at the questions, What, precisely, are the things that are most appropriately exchanged on the market? And what kinds of organization are appropriate for producing and delivering other goods? Civilized nations decided comparatively recently that human beings should not be traded on the market, and so have abolished the sort of property title to persons that can be bought and sold. However, many lesser kinds of property in people's activities, entitlements and liberties remain. It is a serious question whether or not these ought to be abolished.

For the market libertarian any restriction on freedom of exchange is suspect. The libertarian insists that people should, as far as possible, be able to do what they want to do. An important part of their doing what they want to do is their exchanging some of their possessions for others they desire more. Any socially imposed restriction on their opportunities for exchange limits their capacity to realize their desires. Our desires call for the co-operation of others. There are only three ways in which that co-operation can be secured, by coercion, by making it worth the other's while, or by the other voluntarily agreeing to our desires. If coercion is excluded and voluntary agreement is rare, exchange must be the normal method of securing the co-operation of others.

Exchange involves the alienation of entitlements. I alienate my property and it becomes yours, most obviously in the case of material commodities, less obviously in the case of labour power, one's capacity to work for a specified time. The Marxist critique of exchange sees this alienation of property as the reason for rejecting exchange. Exchange leads to a concentration of natural and produced resources in the hands of a few. The majority have nothing to exchange but their labour power, which they cannot use themselves because they have no property in the resources necessary for production. So they must sell their labour power. It will only be bought if the buyers can make a profit out of it, selling its contribution to products for considerably more than they pay for it.

Marx assumed that workers would want to abolish every vestige of a competitive market in labour power. His reason was basically simple. Workers sell their labour power only because they cannot get access to the means of production. If they could themselves take charge of the whole productive process they would cut out the capitalist and end exploitation. They might not be dramatically better off in terms of consumption. Resources would still need to be saved for investment and public purposes. But they would control their own destinies and their own labour. But Marx's conclusion depends on a number of additional premises, as he himself recognized. Granting the labour theory of value and the theory of exploitation, it is still unclear that workers would always object to being exploited, providing there were compensating factors. It is not uncommon, for example, for tradesmen who own their own tools and have enough working capital to set up on their own account to prefer to work for a contractor, in order to have a stable if smaller income, and relief from the anxieties and problems of running their own business.

The task that Marx sets himself in *Capital* is precisely to show that the system of capitalist exploitation cannot be sufficiently stable and benign to allow the working class to accept their exploitation. In the short run, as far as the workers in advanced industrial countries are concerned, Marx's hopes have not been realized.

What many workers want is genuine freedom of choice in selling their labour power, protection against severe competition from cheap labour and reasonable security of employment rather than the abolition of all market relations. They have used their industrial and political power to regulate the package of labour power that is sold to employers, limiting the length of the working day, regulating conditions of work, establishing unemployment relief and various forms of protectionism. The question is whether the result is not to maximize the worst effects of each mechanism, the worst controls and the worst markets. The accusations are often made that the web of controls distorts the market allocation of capital by making productive investment less profitable than manipulation of controls and that labour is rewarded not on the basis of its usefulness but in proportion to its political power. There is clearly some justice in these accusations.

The problem, then, is whether some integral restriction on the development of commodity exchange might avert both capitalist exploitation and the cumbrous systems of state intervention that protect, moderate and direct it. The obvious answer is to prevent the private control of capital by vesting it directly in public trustees, while retaining a free market in labour and its products. If the system were to retain the flexibility and scope for initiative of a market economy the trustee bodies would have to be numerous, independent and competitive. There is clearly a crucial problem in deciding how these trustees are to be appointed and controlled. For the moment let us leave that aside and look at the tasks they would need to accomplish.

II MARKETS IN LAND, MONEY, LABOUR AND COMMODITIES

Land

Land, taken in its most general sense of natural resources, including the sea, the air and the biological resources of the planet, is the condition of all wealth. It is inherently limited in quantity and is often destroyed in use. The system of ownership of land based on first occupancy used to be defended on the ground that there was adequate unused land for those who were willing to face the task of bringing virgin land into production.[4] But now that all the land has been claimed the original common right of access to land must reassert itself, at least to some degree. Those who deny this are led to deny that anybody has a right to life or the means of living.[5] All that one has is a right to compete for them. That the competition is very unequal because some enter the game with plenty of land and others have nothing with which to compete seems not to disturb these authors. I do not think that anybody would embrace this barbarous doctrine were she or he not convinced that once one grants a right to life there follow all kinds of rights, that can only end in the worst sort of 'socialism' or state despotism.

My task is to show that that is not the only alternative. Nevertheless, there are real difficulties here. If a nation increases its population to the point where it can no longer feed it, has it a right to the less intensively used land of its neighbour? What is the relevant group here? Has the individual a right to self-sufficiency on his own land, or the family, or the clan? What is special about the nation? On the other hand, according to the different technologies and patterns of consumption that individuals and groups adopt, they will have very different needs for diverse resources. Clearly they cannot have all the resources needed for just any lifestyle they happen to want. If resources are vested in geographically defined communities the easiest way to allow more equal access of all to natural resources – both productive resources and natural amenities – is by breaking down barriers to migration. But unrestricted migration would pose enormous problems, and, in the short run at least, be terribly disruptive.

There is no question of attempting to provide solutions to all these problems here. In time, given appropriate social changes, many of them could be mitigated. People would not want to migrate given freer trade, access to raw materials at prices they could pay and an adequate living space at home. The tendency of families and nations to procreate inordinately is largely an effect of poverty, insecurity and poor standards of child welfare and education. The question is not one of finding an equitable basis for *dividing up* property in land and resources between rival claimants but of finding ways in which appropriate opportunities to make *use* of scarce resources can be as widely available as possible. Just as importantly, resources must continue to be available to future generations. Enough of the earth's topsoil and other irreplaceable resources has already been destroyed. The task must also be one of conservation.

What these considerations suggest is that the trustees of various natural resources might discharge their functions by making them available to anybody who wished to use them at prices sufficiently high to discourage their being used frivolously, and under strict conditions about conservation. As far as possible these trustees would be required to provide jointly enough revenue for public purposes to make taxation largely unnecessary. The common heritage of human beings would meet the basic costs of social security for all. So the problem of all benefiting from the use of natural resources would be largely solved, provided, of course, the most important resources were available to people anywhere in the world on acceptable terms.

In order to see how such a goal might be achieved it is essential to rid oneself of traditional notions of sovereignty. Instead we must envisage specialized authorities each entrusted with specific authority to regulate the use of some particular resource in a suitably defined area. One authority might regulate use of farming land, another forests, another fossil fuels, another various mineral resources, another water supplies, and so on. These authorities would need to be co-ordinated with each other within a given area so that mining would be reconciled with agriculture, water collection and storage with both and so on. At the same time they would need to be co-ordinated with other authorities of the same type in other areas to ensure a coherent policy of use of fossil fuels, of minerals, of agricultural soil and so on, ideally on a world scale. Finally, the revenues derived by each of these authorities would need to be disbursed in a co-ordinated way to provide for needs that are currently met by taxation, not just for inhabitants of the territory in which they happen to be situated but for all those who need the relevant assistance.

Obviously, to achieve such multi-dimensional co-ordination on a world scale by means of a central world organization would involve a colossal concentration of power, an extremely complex bureaucracy and an enormous complex of laws and regulations. There is no possibility of such a complex being controlled democratically. The distance between the individual voters and the ultimate decision-makers would be too great. It would seem to be inevitable that the bureaucracy would use its power in its own interests and that something like the so-called 'Asiatic mode of production' on a world scale would result. Rigid and stringent control, surveillance and repression would be necessary to ensure that all regional chauvinism was eliminated. We could have peace and security at the price of a static, uniform and inefficient social order.

The central authorities would be in a position to regulate almost all activities. If they were wise in their self-interest the result might be a considerable degree of security, equality and perhaps even contentment of a sort for most of humankind. It might come out quite well on a Benthamite calculus of pleasures and pains and even on some formal moralities of a Kantian kind. It might even be the case that people would come to accept it willingly. Given suitable technology it might not demand too much of them. They might have a great deal of leisure and accept the constraint of the system as the price of a life of ease and of play.

Such a world state is not all that unlikely a development. If a sufficiently ruthless and far-sighted nation-state were to gain absolute military superiority it would almost certainly be in its interest to force the development of a world-state by a gradual process of setting up and enforcing adherence to a number of international authorities over which it could exercise ultimate control. Each step might be a small enough diminution of sovereignty, and in the interests of enough of its vassals, not to provoke too much revolt. Only the first steps would be difficult.

It is not surprising that those who want to preserve diversity and flexibility in social life and minimize the role of uncontrolled authorities are afraid of making any concessions to the principles of common use of natural resources. It is, as we shall see later, very doubtful whether any stringent conception of distributive justice or equality could be put into practice without an all-embracing authority to establish and enforce it. If we do not want rigidity some looser form of co-ordination and regulation of the use of resources is needed.

What I want to suggest is that there might be a suitable kind of co-ordination and regulation on the basis of largely voluntary negotiation and co-operation between the trustees of various resources. The key problem is to ensure that such trustees are responsive not just to the needs of the present but of the future, and not just to the desires of the inhabitants of the immediate vicinity of the land they are entrusted with but to the needs of all those who have a claim on its use. If this responsiveness is to be assured the members of the board of trustees must be representative of the wide group of people who have a legitimate interest in the way in which it is used. They must be in a position to resist the pressures to sacrifice future needs to present interests, and they must have adequate motivation to do so, in co-operation with other similar or cognate bodies.

My contention is that these requirements can be achieved if the members of these boards are chosen so as to be statistically representative of those with an interest in their decisions,[6] and if the principal reward attached to their work is long-term recognition of the soundness of their decisions. That recognition will be well based and valued if it comes in the first instance from their colleagues and successors on their own and cognate bodies. It will be the main reward if the proceedings of these bodies are thoroughly public and widely reported in a form that invites public comment, so that corruption and misrepresentation are unlikely to succeed and will be punished if detected. It will be adequate reward if the society generally attaches great value to effective public service.

In order to ensure that they have a positive interest in serving those chosen will have to be volunteers. In order to ensure that they do not form an entrenched group they will not be subject to re-appointment to the same office. Continuity would be assured by replacing members one at a time at a suitable interval rather than as a group all at the same time. The period of office of members would need to be long enough to make it worth their while to go to the trouble of getting to know a great deal about the problems involved. To ensure flexibility, initiative and responsibility each group of trustees would have a free hand and not be subject to policy directions from any superior authority. Nor would individual members be formally subject to any directions from those whom they were chosen to represent. Their accountability to a constituency would be entirely a matter of the force of opinions and informal sanctions; decisions that were outrageous would not be obeyed by those affected.

It would be expected of the various trustee bodies that they would set up co-ordinating bodies of a specialized nature to ensure a satisfactory interrelation of decisions as they affected other bodies. Such co-ordinating bodies would be in a position to bring strong pressure against merely idiosyncratic or chauvinist decisions. In addition various voluntary organizations would campaign for the adoption of particular standards and policies. They would be analogous to the organizations that now represent various community groups and lobby for their interests.

None of these things would ensure equal regard for all individuals and interest groups or uniformity of provisions for handling problems.[7] The decisions of the various bodies would represent compromises between conflicting pressures, needs and aspirations. They would have to make unpopular decisions, increasing the price of resources to ration them and to generate funds for public purposes, often against the short-term interests of communities that are used to regarding those resources as their own. They would have to accept that very often the rightness of their decisions could not be demonstrated in the short term. They would try not to push change so quickly as to provoke revolt while responding as quickly as possible to the most important considerations. They would try to represent not the unreflecting desires of people but their long-term interests and those of generations to come.

From an economic point of view the prices charged for natural resources would be monopoly prices. They would feed into the price system as a largely exogenously determined variable. Nevertheless, the relative prices charged for competing resources, for example, oil and coal, would reflect market response to prices, as well as other considerations such as the environmental costs of say strip mining as opposed to drilling. There are already monopoly price elements in the prices of most natural resources, even when there are no concerted attempts to constitute a monopoly. Indeed, in so far as they are pure rents or simply returns for ownership rights, all such prices are monopoly prices, since they depend on the exclusive power of ownership. In this respect natural resources are contrasted sharply with products that can be reproduced at will by human labour and whose qualities depend on the quality of the labour put into them. My labour is mine in a way my land cannot be.

Moreover, many of the advantages of any given piece of agricultural land and almost all the advantages of any piece of land for commercial or residential building are the creation of public expenditure or of private expenditure by people other than the owner of the land in question. There is no good reason why, as Henry George argued, the whole value that accrues to land through its social situation should not belong to society. There is no reason why the aggregate revenue from letting land should not be very substantial, covering the costs of most public services. The difficulties in introducing such a system are enormous, but it is the sort of change that could be made gradually, and the problems solved piecemeal, if there were sufficient support for it.

The abolition of private ownership of land would, of course, remove an important source of unearned income and the very wasteful diversion of time and resources into speculative investment in real estate and natural resources.

Money

In so far as money itself is a commodity it commands interest, a charge simply for the use of money for a certain time. In part the ability of money to command a price is a function of its relative scarcity. There are always people who want things now for which they cannot now pay, but hope to be able to pay in the future. Other people who want to keep money for the future are prepared to lend it now for a consideration. Some of those who want money now are consumers, who are in effect prepared to pay more to have what they want now than they would have to pay if they waited until they had saved enough money. Others are producers who can make enough profit out of the investment of borrowed money to more than cover the cost of borrowing it.

A variety of financial institutions serve as agents in the process of matching lenders and borrowers, assuming risks and spreading them over a large range of transactions so as to minimize them, and organizing asset backing against loans. Such institutions lend not only money that they actually possess but money that they hope to possess as a result of interest payments, repayments of existing loans and new deposits. They create credit. The creation of credit is always potentially inflationary. There is wide agreement that it needs to be controlled and that the state seems to be the only effective agency for controlling it. However, states themselves are borrowers who are under a very strong temptation to print money to finance their own operations. So they must in turn be controlled by an international monetary system that attempts to prevent them from creating too much credit, basically by refusing to accept their money at face value if it is inflated. The system is notoriously weak because the political consequences of bankrupting a nation state are too high to contemplate.

At every level the monetary system favours the larger and wealthier unit against the smaller. The firm, the individual, the country with large assets and strong production resources can normally borrow relatively more money and on better terms than the smaller or poorer unit, quite independently of their respective needs for either productive investment or consumption. The credit system leads to a concentration of further power in the already powerful. Moreover, governments and major institutions are reluctant to face the consequences of any large institution being bankrupted. So such institutions are commonly given assistance when they get into difficulties that is not given to smaller institutions. Their power is correspondingly entrenched, their risks minimized and their incentive to grow reinforced. All of this, of course, imposes costs that are born ultimately by workers and consumers.

As the mass of entrenched money grows the more or less fixed and guaranteed entitlements to interest and service payments on that money grows. The costs that have to be met before an enterprise can make a profit increase. So that these disincentives to investment do not choke economic activity a range of concessions must be introduced, special allowances for depreciation, subsidies, protective tariffs and so on. These in turn have to be paid for, increasing the rate of taxation and so on. For a while inflation helps ease the situation by reducing the rate of real interest on money, but the power of money reasserts itself to demand its due. Inflation encourages destabilizing speculation that must be curbed if the system is to survive. Nevertheless, astute operations in the money market are often much more profitable than productive investment.

There are two radical proposals for dealing with this state of affairs, the installation of a ruthless system of *laissez-faire* capitalism, in which all political protection for capital is removed, and some form of 'socialization' of capital in the hands of the state. Both are radically unsatisfactory. The *laissez-faire* solution provide no way of keeping the state from interfering, granted that captalism tends to crises and both capital and labour will demand that it intervene, reinforcing the state's own tendency to increase the range of its activities.

Moreover, it fails to address itself to the point that capitalism itself generates central financial institutions of enormous power that have an interest in acting in concert rather than competitively to protect their power.[8] State socialism involves the centralization of initiative, bureaucracy and insensitivity to consumer needs. It offers workers and enterprises a certain security at the cost of liberty and openness to change.

It would be possible to get the best of both proposals, without the most obvious disadvantages of either, if the major monetary resources of the community were vested in a variety of institutions that were constrained by market requirements but motivated in directing investment by a more comprehensive set of considerations than the market can reflect. Such institutions would grant or lend for production and consumption primarily on their assessment of the relative social utility of those investments, subject to the requirement that their lending be reasonably safe and not inflationary. Their lending would need to be co-ordinated by agreement among themselves and regulated by appropriate rules. Much the same patterns for constituting such bodies would be employed as were sketched out for trustees of natural resources.

The difficulties of ensuring that trustees of money act responsibly are, however, very much more serious than those of controlling the trustees of natural resources. And the tasks facing the trustees are very much more complex and difficult. The root of these difficulties is the general exchangeability of money and the range of economic functions it performs. A specific piece of farmland or a mineral right has a limited number of practicable uses in a given economy, and the consequences of using it in most of these ways will be fairly clear, granted that the relevant scientific knowledge is available. The trustees have a relatively precise problem to deal with. On the other hand, if they only have a certain amount of money, what criteria are to guide them in choosing among the infinity of things that can be done with it? How are all the independent decisions of trustee bodies to be co-ordinated?

There is no abstract solution to the problem. Historically, however, any functioning modern economy will have a variety of financial institutions with a range of explicit and implicit commitments to customers and to other institutions. A beginning could be made by injecting social requirements into the market by agreements among those bodies about the rate of interest for various types of loans, the sort of bodies that are to be eligible for loans or other support and so on. The amount of a given currency in circulation and the money supply generally might still be managed by a reserve bank operating independently of any state authority.

Fundamental overall co-ordination would still be secured by the market. However, the preferences expressed in this market would not only be those of people in possession of money, but also those of interests that cannot rely on private money, the interests of children and the yet to be born, community interests in public goods and the needs of people with special problems. Still there are problems about private accumulation of money as long as money means power. It is not enough to feed into the market all those needs that are not adequately reflected in the effective (cash-backed) demand of individual consumers. There is also the problem that some individuals or firms may have such a strong position in a sector of the market because of their wealth that their preferences dominate it.

Let us suppose, for example, that as a result of a revolution, state power has been used to expropriate most large concentrations of wealth and vest them in trustee bodies working in a market economy, and that the state power is subsequently abolished. There then seems to be nothing to prevent the people accumulating wealth except competition and social pressure. There is now no authority that can confiscate such wealth in virtue of its sovereignty. The legitimate power to confiscate is a state power, if anything is, and if we are serious about getting rid of the state that power must go. If we allow state power to confiscate it will be politically impossible to prevent the dynamics of state power from re-emerging.

Are there ways in which a community of trustee-controlled economic agencies could prevent the emergence of large concentrations of privately owned wealth, or at least contain their economic effects within fairly narrow bounds? Undoubtedly they could if they were to co-operate amongst themselves. They could restrict the access of private corporations to natural resources and credit, for example, in cases where this seemed desirable. They could subsidize competition against certain corporations where they enjoyed a monopolistic or oligopolistic position. Such practices would be discriminatory, and according to some conceptions of justice, unjust. In the short run they might also be economically inefficient. But they could be effective, and in the long run economically justified. Even if they did involve an economic cost, the political good of preventing the excessive concentration of social power based on private wealth could be worth it.

The trustee bodies would be likely to reach agreement about practical plans of this sort only if there were a substantial consensus about the dangers to be avoided and the ways of meeting them. Such agreement would have to rest on objective and thorough analysis. A mere politics of envy would be unstable and blind. The point would not be to bring about some arbitrarily determined equality of wealth but to avert concentration of power that might endanger the public control of major economic resources. So the community might be quite tolerant of people amassing wealth for deferred private consumption or for purposes that were public in character, such as the promotion of some sport or the arts or even some unpopular set of ideas. It would certainly be dangerous if a consortium of trustee bodies arrogated to themselves the function of imposing particular moral ideals on everybody. Their function would basically be to attempt to feed into the market mechanism relevant public needs and to use their power against concrete threats to the system. I shall return to the question of public morality later.

What I am suggesting, then, is a compromise between market-libertarian and socialist means of allocating wealth to productive purposes and controlling the distribution of the product. There is no suggestion that such a compromise would be ideal, but merely that it could work and could provide a solution to contemporary problems, if only it could be brought about. In particular it would not, once established, require anybody to exercise state-like powers. It would have the sort of allocative efficiency that is claimed for competitive markets, with the proviso that some prices and conditions of use of resources would be set monopolistically. These monopolies would be justified as the means of expressing certain social preferences that could not be expressed effectively in the market in any other way. The trustees of these monopolies would be representative of the people affected by their decisions and responsive to informed public debate. Social control of resources would be doubly mediated, by the market and by the democratic process.

The compromise would not satisfy those socialists who object to market relationships not only because of the concentrations of power and consequent exploitation that they generate but because of the kind of people and of social relationships that they produce. I shall discuss this objection more fully later. For the moment it is sufficient to remark that nobody thinks that market relationships can be abolished overnight. If market relationships are to be abolished there is no doubt that the way to start is by attempting to remove natural resources and capital from purely private control. The scheme I have outlined shows how this might work without the state and without attempting to replace the market with some unspecified means of social decision-making. Moreover, it is open to development towards a fuller form of socialism if associations are formed that gradually extend the areas in which free co-operation replaces market competition.

Labour

I have argued that in regard to land and money the market could be modified so as to feed into it as monopoly prices and conditions of use those socially desirable requirements that are not otherwise reflected in market prices. The ground for the exercise of such monopoly power on behalf of the community is that wealth is to a large extent a product of the community, that its possession confers great power which needs to be controlled, and that there are interests, especially those of future generations, that can be protected in no other way. Moreover, making wealth, natural resources or money, available on the open market to all at prices and under conditions set with an eye to the public interest seems a sensible and equitable way of assuring they will be well used. The specific use is up to the entrepreneurs, whether they be workers' co-operatives or individuals, so that decentralized initiative is preserved. The success or failure of enterprise depends on the market. There is no need for further regulation.

But what of labour itself? Is it not also a product of the community that has educated it? The community has produced and transmitted the culture, technology and relationships that labour depends on in operation, and that give it its meaning and value. What is done with labour affects the future of the community just as surely as what is done with land or money. 'Human capital', it is said, is 'our greatest resource.' Is it not, then, equally necessary that it be so directed that it is used for common purposes? Moreover, talents are very unequally distributed. If we are going to refuse to allow accidents of inheritance to influence the access of people to natural resources and money, is it not equally appropriate that labour too should be pooled, according to the maxim 'From each according to ability, to each according to need'?

Such a pooling of labour is both possible and natural in small communities where the ties of mutual interdependence are strong and readily visible, where the contribution of each person to the life of the community is constantly being appraised by others and where there is little disagreement about what the contribution of each should be. The range of common goods is small but each person shares in the decisions, the work and the results. The individual counts significantly, having a say, making a substantial contribution to the work force and to the enjoyment of the results. The larger the scale, the less the mechanism on which community depends can operate flexibly and the less satisfaction they can provide to most of the participants. Requirements become regularized and systematized. Routine replaces challenge, the individual becomes a cog in a machine, required to grind on reliably. Organization designed for efficiency removes all the variability, wealth of random communication and mutual interest that make a community.

To socialize labour by subjecting it to organization radically destroys small communities and thus destroys the possibility of a discipline that is not simply oppressive. So contract and enforcement of contract replace role and role-satisfaction as the social basis of work for common goals for most people, at least outside the ambit of friendships and family relationships. One sells one's labour on the market for the best price one can get, alienating it for a specified time in exchange for the money one needs to live one's personal life in freedom. Let us prescind, for the moment, from exploitation, from the fact that people are normally forced to sell their labour power for less than the value of its product. There are still many repulsive features in this situation. Kinds of labour are rewarded roughly in proportion to the amount of training and experience they require, even though much of that training and experience has been at community expense. Most jobs are insecure. A person can be dismissed without any failure on his or her part and without regard to the effects of dismissal on the person's life. There is a continual struggle over the price of labour power which is also destructive in many of its effects on people and their relationships.

Nevertheless, in a large-scale society there seems no acceptable alternative to the wage contract as the basis of social coordination of labour. What can be done to ameliorate it? It would seem that the most desirable situation would be one in which everybody was assured of a minimal living whether they chose to work or not. The inducement to work would be a combination of the interest of the work and the rewards for doing things that people wanted to be done but did not want to do. In such circumstances one might expect a great variety of arrangements to emerge as people chose the sort of contracts that suited their interests, some seeking immediate monetary return, others long-term returns, others job-satisfaction and so on. In such a market one would expect the most unpleasant jobs to be the most highly paid, and prestigious and interesting jobs to attract little extrinsic remuneration.

Those who chose not to sell their labour on the market would not necessarily be a social burden. They might participate in different voluntary associations for whatever purposes they preferred. The activities of many of these associations would enrich the life of the community beyond their membership, as so many sporting, cultural, humanitarian, educational and political associations now do. In these associations the role of money would be reduced as far as possible by switching labour to relatively costless goods, that is to say, goods that provide sufficient rewards to the supplier in most circumstances to ensure that there will be an abundant supply. The existence of such a varied community life presupposes a variety of readily accessible material facilities, many of which would have to be supplied as common goods; libraries, computing facilities, playing fields, halls and perhaps communications equipment.

The achievement of such a state of affairs is conditional on further substantial increases in the productivity of paid labour coupled with a substantial shift in demand away from products where labour is a cost towards those where it is, in appropriate circumstances, a benefit. A forced rise in the price of natural resources would probably assist this change, since there is a strong association between unpleasant labour and industries that involve a high use of natural resources. So, for example, people might get used to communicating electronically rather than travelling, using durable and repairable rather than throwaway goods, and using self-renewing or recycled resources rather than mining the earth. The object would be to transfer much work back to local and domestic settings and small co-operative groups where it would form part of a micro-economy of mutual assistance.

The most important economic difficulty in this scenario is that it would make food and housing relatively much more costly, since food production and distribution and building are such heavy users of fuel, soil and minerals, as well as of a good deal of unpleasant labour. Obviously it is very difficult to supply relatively costly items as free goods. Ultimately the labour costs have to be borne by those who work in the money economy. We seem to be caught in a contradiction. Suppose the non-monetary economy is highly successful in supplying most people with satisfying activities. In that case few will work for money and then only for a high return. The result will be that it will be impossible to sustain the supply of food, housing and material services. The rewards for under-taking the unpleasant work on which these goods depend will tend to eat into the product, increasing its price and making it impossible to sustain free support to those who do not do 'productive' work. On the other hand, very many people may not be satisfied with the sort of life that can be sustained mainly by the non-monetary goods. In that case they will try very hard to reduce the price of monetary goods. They will not consent to high prices for natural resources and they will be caught in a struggle over the price of various kinds of labour, attempting to raise the price of labour they find congenial or for which they are equipped and lower the price of all other labour. They will try to reverse the policies on which the free supply of public goods depends. In a democratic polity they may prevail.

The dilemma is serious, though not necessarily fatal to the project. There may be points of fairly stable equilibrium for very highly productive economies with diverse populations in which there is a rough balance of power between the forces that tend to undercut monetary rewards too drastically and those that tend to increase them at the expense of natural and common resources. Such a balance of forces would be the easier to maintain in proportion as the variety of forces on each side are dispersed and unable to bring consolidated pressure to bear on the outcome.[9]

Short of paying people a wage even if they do not engage in production for the market, there are other possibilities. Granted some generous assistance for the disadvantaged, a social insurance scheme that was both compulsory and 'progressive' in its incidence would go some way towards securing the same object. One would qualify for benefits only on the basis of past contributions or one's willingness to work at whatever job was offered. It would, of course, be easy to use such a scheme to conscript people for work in any situation where employment was hard to get. So unions would try to insist on minimum wages and conditions of employment, in effect preventing the market from driving down the price of labour power, in spite of its oversupply. Libertarian economists insist that the effect of such restrictions is to make employing the unemployed less attractive. And so it does. Unfortunately for the unemployed, there are kinds of labour that a given market does not want at any price, and it is not always possible for labour to change its skills and capabilities. But the market pressure for those who can change to do so cannot be relaxed too much or its effectiveness in allocating labour will be impaired.

So once again we are in a conflict that admits of no stable resolution. The free market is attractive to the extent that one has a genuine choice about what to sell and what to buy. The worker without reserves is in the position of having to accept whatever price is offered or whatever conditions are attached to unemployment assistance. The interests of employers lie in driving down that price, and by and large employers do have reserves. At worst they can spend their capital. But supplying the worker with adequate reserves to tide him or her over the period of unemployment tends to reverse the advantage in favour of the worker. If there is no particular pressure on the worker to retrain or relocate how is change to be brought about in the interests of efficiency? The difficulty is not resolved by making the workers corporately their own employer. The question is not just one of the allocation of resources between workers as consumer and producers. It is mainly a question of work among workers. In so far as that question is decided by the political power of fractions within the working population there will always be conflict about how much protection from market forces is to be given to any one section of the workforce. For ultimately that protection has to be paid for by the insurance premiums that fall on the rest.

Such issues must be made into issues of equity rather than relative power, not only for the sake of equity but for the sake of reasonable security and stability for individuals, groups and the community as a whole. So there must be a judicial rather than a political approach to questions of what are fair conditions of work.[10] The decisions will have to be in terms of community standards of fairness of opportunity, having consideration for the needs of all concerned and the good functioning of a free market. Such judgements would proceed not by the application of rigid standards but by piecemeal adjustments of entitlements in the light of problems that arose and of conceptions of what constitutes desirable change.

Once again I would urge that if these decisions fell to representative committees charged with disbursing public funds it should be possible, granted a suitable degree of social consensus, for acceptable judgements to be made and secure acceptance without recourse to state power. In addition to securing a livelihood for those the market does not want to employ and a genuine choice for those who can be employed, systems that offer a reasonable livelihood even to those who do not produce marketable commodities would be efficient in economic terms in distributing labour that was offered on the market. There would be less pressure to feather-bedding, more willingness on the part of workers to accept diverse and flexible conditions of employment, and perhaps a more stable consumer demand. Such a market might serve as a stepping-stone towards transcending market relationships if the non-market sector of the economy in which people produce public goods for the joy of it gradually subsumed more and more labour.

We are all willing to do difficult and unpleasant things when they are an integral part of some overall task that is highly rewarding. The essential thing is that the connection between the unpleasant elements and the overall achievement be close and personal. Such close connections can be preserved only in small groups where a team spirit can be sustained. Communitarians have rightly emphasized that the crucial social change that needs to be made in overcoming commodity relations in the case of labour is the reconstruction of production so as to institute teamwork rather than atomized relationships as the typical form of the organization of work. Considerable technological ingenuity will be called for in many cases, But in most it is mainly a matter of getting rid of the bureaucratic imperative for control from above in favour of more 'horizontal' kinds of co-ordination.

Commodities and consumption

One of the central features of the philosophical background and practical force of the 'mixed' economy that I am advocating is the rejection of any uniformity of moral ideals. There do, of course, have to be generally accepted moral prohibitions and duties that are enforced by public opinion. But these would relate only to a minimal morality. There are some questions about which substantial disagreements ought to be possible without fracturing the basic moral unity of the society. For instance, What characteristics are better or more praiseworthy or more important? What balance is to be struck between self-interest and altruism? What others have most claim on benevolence? and What sort of striving for ideals is desirable?

So it should be possible without too much difficulty to construct for oneself a relatively solitary existence or to form a highly integrated commune, to work very hard and accumulate personal wealth for consumption or to promote some end of one's own or to live in relative security with a minimum of possessions. There is no way in which such a variety of lifestyles can be accommodated without a great variety of goods being available in the form of commodities. What one would hope is that in a society where everybody was assured of the basic necessities of life on conditions that were not very onerous, and in which there was ample opportunity for everybody who wanted to participate in public life, the symbolic importance of commodities as status symbols would decline. They would become purely instrumental to practical purposes. Granted a rich community life there would be plenty of other kinds of satisfaction available.

Nevertheless, there is no reason for believing that even in a dominantly communitarian culture desires for personal wealth would disappear. I believe that it is essential that they not be suppressed but be given ample opportunity for fulfilment under suitable conditions. Attempts to force conformity to a communitarian ideal guarantee that personal acquisitiveness and ambition will find hypocritcal expression in the pursuit of ostensibly altruistic goals. Providing these desires with legitimate and accessible forms of fulfilment is at least a condition of keeping them from dominating public life. If people are prepared to pay the price the community demands for the use of the means of acquiring wealth they should be able to do so. One may want to buy a yacht and sail around the world, another to acquire a house with a beautiful view, another to set up some project that no public body is prepared to support. Others may simply want to show that they are smarter than their competitors.

Again, the existence of commodity relations is the condition of free and flexible communal consumption by voluntary associations. No smorgasbord can cater for every taste. There are enormous differences in cost in satisfying diverse tastes, whether they be individual or collective. One commune will want a swimming pool, a sauna, a garden and a children's playground. Another will sacrifice these things in favour of an inner-city location. The only way in which these various demands can be reconciled and costed is by the market. A great variety of amenities ranging from pleasant outlooks to building hardware to caviar have to be available as commodities. Correspondingly, as we have already seen, the labour by which people earn entitlements to these things must also be traded as a commodity.

We already know that commodity relationships and communal relationships can coexist. Every family, every voluntary association and every political movement offers instances of people who in some of their relationships work for common goals and in others for purely personal gain. No doubt the preponderance of egoistic behaviour may need to be redressed. But we are talking about a change of emphasis not a radical moral and social conversion.

Nothing can alter the fact that in any society short of paradisal abundance many people will have some unsatisfied desires and that the easiest way of satisfying them will be by such means as theft, misrepresentation, extortion and corruption. No doubt commodity relationships often encourage desires and make it easier to employ immoral means to satisfy them. Any foreseeable society is going to have the problem of preventing and rectifying crime. But what is of particular significance to the sort of society I am advocating is that the various public bodies be on the whole incorruptible, and do not become instruments of theft, extortion and oppression.

In the main my proposal relies on the fact that their membership is chosen by lot, changed regularly, and obliged to conduct all its proceedings in ways that are open to public scrutiny, especially the scrutiny of their predecessors and of those who hope to be chosen for office. Such scrutiny, however, can only work to detect systematic misallocation of resources, as opposed to episodic fraud, when the costs and benefits of what is done are clearly established. In the case of most of those costs and benefits there is no way of quantifying them except through market prices. No other sort of quantitative measure will do, because what has to be established is not some natural property of the things in question but how much effective demand there is for them. Even where goods are not directly marketable their value has to be established in relation to things that have a market price if any straightforward cost-benefit analysis is to be possible.

This is not to suggest that cost-benefit analysis based on market pricing is even in principle the ideal form of rational decision procedure for the allocation of resources. It is not, in my view, even in those ideal situations pictured in economists' models, for it is by no means obvious that it is entirely sensible, granted the sort of beings that we are, to try to be 'rational' in the economist's sense. Nor is it always morally desirable. The point simply is that even when we depart from it we need some common bench-mark that can be clearly established if we are to be clear about the way in which different proposals are to be compared.

There are many grounds on which one can argue that a specific cost-benefit analysis should be overridden. But few of these will be absolute prohibitions. Usually it is a matter of weighing something that is not directly quantifiable against something that the market can put a price on. Such unique and inalienable things as traditions, sentiments and friend-ships cannot be priced. But there may be prices that we are not prepared to pay to preserve them. It is desirable that we face such issues clearly, especially in public life. Not to do so is to encourage deception, mystification and manipulation, to ask to be deceived and defrauded.

It may well be that in time we shall discover other and better ways of accommodating a large variety of diverse preferences than by market relationships. Until we do we cannot have any *positive* reason for thinking that communism as the great nineteenth-century founders envisaged it is socially possible. There are, I believe, good reasons for wanting to go in that direction. But we can only go anywhere with the means that we have at hand and that will work within the range of conditions that we can bank on. Revolution does not create new relationships. They emerge out of gradual social change, especially the emergence and diffusion of new practices. New practices can be introduced deliberately only when they can be clearly described and taught. Even then they will not endure unless they become interwoven with the fabric of social practices and social motivations. For the most part we have to build new societies with the methods of the old because there are no other methods that we know how to operate. What is important if we are to change the results of using those old methods, is to change the combinations and circumstances in which they are used.

5
Is demarchy possible?

I THE CONDITIONS OF DEMARCHY

a The first condition of demarchy being possible is that the society in which it is to be instituted be reasonably democratic in its social attitudes. While recognizing that people may differ greatly in particular abilities, the demarchist does not believe that there is any group of people whose capacities entitle them to a position of special or wide-ranging power in the community. At the base level choices made by people of no special ability are likely to be reasonable provided they are based on sound knowledge. They may need expert advice, but the judgement about whose advice to take is appropriately made by lay persons.

b The productive technology of the society must be ample to provide a good deal of time and resources that can be devoted to public debate and decision-making.

c People must value the opportunity for effective participation in matters that interest them and be prepared to leave other matters to those who have those interests, provided they are satisfied that the system is fair and effective.

d People must be anxious to avoid rigidity, bureaucracy and concentration or power. They must want to avoid giving power to the state if other social mechanisms will produce common goods reliably and fairly.

These broad conditions are already secure in the 'advanced' countries of both the 'first' and 'second' worlds. They all profess democratic ideologies and democratic sentiments are deeply grounded in much of the micro-structure of life. They all support enormous military and bureaucratic superstructures and could easily support the costs of demarchy. The tenor of discussion is mostly sensible and tolerant. People do not particularly love the state. It is more difficult to speak about the so-called third world, however. In many cases standards of education and knowledge of the mechanisms of large-scale societies may be lacking, as well as other conditions. It is difficult for a Westerner to be sure. Let us stick to the 'first' and 'second' worlds, which in any case dominate the third world militarily, economically and ideologically.

It is quite striking how easily demarchy can be explained to people without any special acquaintance with political theory, and how readily they can see it as a system that could work once it was instituted. It involves no great assumptions about the possibility of a radical change of consciousness. It does not presuppose a great moral renewal, much as one may hope that it would lead to a stronger and more effective moral sensibility. Most people think that there are enough people already who have the qualities necessary to make the system work. It is not difficult for people to see demarchy as an attractive proposal that might indeed solve many of our socio-economic and political problems. Unfortunately the very simplicity and plausibility of the proposal undercuts it. It is very hard to believe that the answer to our most pressing problems is so simple and so bland.

A movement that would make a 'world-historical' change ought to rest on some great religious revelation or metaphysical world-view, make claims in the name of sacred and inalienable rights, call for vengeance on the oppressors, have colour and drama. It should be complex, mysterious and elusive, allowing many different forces to be harnessed together as each sees in the whole what it longs to see. It ought to have clearly identifiable enemies, people of flesh and blood who can be hated and demons to be exorcized. Its programme should be symbolized in a great symbolic act. At least, so the historical record suggests.

But perhaps the days of that kind of politics are passed. Certainly, it is no longer possible for most mature and reflective people to believe in that kind of vision. Just as, for the most part, we believe that progress in curing the ills of our bodies depends on understanding the specific mechanisms by which they work, so our general experience of social life inclines us to look for particular practical mechanisms to deal with the functional problems of social life. We know better than to take a simple mechanical view of these matters. Beliefs, hopes and fears are important. We know, too, that mechanisms outside the simplest ones of physical mechanics do not have entirely predictable consequences or conditions of operation. Only experience can show their powers and limitations.

In these circumstances one might hope that a significant change in our society's ways of operating might be brought about by convincing people that there are definite procedures that are at least worth trying because they promise to solve many of our most important problems. The great difficulties in bringing about such a change are twofold:

a   The first steps. How are we to get the new procedure a decent trial? Not many people are going to be interested in trying a new form of democracy unless they can be shown instances of its working in practice, not just in some utopian community committed to it on principle, but in normal circumstances.

b   The interests opposed to it. Obviously, if we are proposing to replace all our political elites, most of our bureaucracy and the private ownership of land and large capital, all the ruling strata in society have an interest in opposing us. It seems too much to hope that one could fight all of these opponents at the same time and win.

The two difficulties are closely intertwined with each other. They cannot be met head on, but only obliquely, and only with a good deal of luck. What I hope is that it may be possible to get the process started by finding areas of responsibility where the present ways of doing things manifestly fail. It will be in the interests of those who bear the stigma of that failure to try to get rid of those responsibilities to whatever institutions are willing to accept them. One of the great virtues of demarchy is that it can, unlike centralized forms of socialism, be introduced in a piecemeal way, provided there is sufficient agreement that it is worth trying in a particular area. Even where centralized socialism now exists it is possible that the powers that be may find demarchically constituted bodies an attractive solution to the problem of making concessions to demands for decentralization and democracy without the threats to stability that electoral democracy entails in such a situation. Demarchy might minimize fuss and provide a gradual transition to a more democratic society.

It is not unusual for authorities to foster institutions that, if they were to grow, would threaten their power. Often they are seeking a counterbalance to an immediate threat, buying support, placating discontent or putting off the day of reckoning. Often they assume that the new institutions could never grow into a substantial threat. It was inconceivable to the monarchs of the *ancien régime* that mere merchants and manufacturers might usurp their authority. No doubt our present politicians and bureaucrats see themselves as functionally irreplaceable. In a sense they are, as long as their functions are reproduced by the practices in which things get done. Any authority with this sort of confidence in itself is open to a process of attrition. It is willing to let go specific areas of power for immediate and tangible gains, thinking thereby to secure its ultimate authority. In the long run, however, an authority that is only an ultimate authority is powerless. Everything is decided before it can intervene. The cost of overturning what is already decided are too great. Often the authority no longer has the capacity to generate positive alternatives. It makes a show of doing something, but is really a rubber stamp.

II STRATEGIES OF CHANGE

Where, then, can we make a start in this process of undermining existing power structures without confronting them? One obvious place is in the general areas of health, education and welfare. Contemporary capitalism is at the moment conducting a very successful counter-offensive against the growth of the welfare state, abetted by popular discontent with bureaucracy and high levels of taxation. That offensive is unlikely to have much long-term success once its results become manifest. Once the quality of health care, education and other services available to the ordinary voter declines dramatically there will be a reaction. Private medicine and education have become extremely costly as the private bureaucracies of the health insurance industry join with the professions to increase the slice of the GNP that the industry as a whole appropriates.

Both private and state supply and control of these goods breed bureaucracy and high costs. In either case people are going to demand better value for their money. The demand is going to focus on the state, because even if it can extricate itself to some extent from supplying these goods, it is inextricably implicated in controlling their production. The professions and the institutions through which they operate exist in their monopoly forms only through a great network of legal and administrative provisions ranging from licences to practice to tax deductions, drug regulations and assignments of professional responsibility. They everywhere depend on substantial public subsidies, tax concessions and facilities.

Faced with responsibilities they cannot evade but cannot meet, it must be very tempting for politicians to attempt to off-load some of their tasks on to institutions for which they are not responsible. The obvious move is to turn them over to existing lower-level local authorities, states, provinces, countries or municipalities. But this move produces neither better service nor much less bureaucracy nor reduced costs. The higher authorities cannot escape all responsibility since there is already an established practice of their making grants for such purposes to lower-level authorities. Neither authority wants the responsibility under the conditions which the other imposes. Neither can evade it. So it is tempting for both to look for a third party on which to impose the burden.

In these circumstances it might appear quite attractive to harassed politicians to arrive at a fixed formula for funding entirely independent agencies to take care of the problems. One way of making clear that these agencies were entirely independent and governed by those directly involved as producers and consumers would be to put them under demarchical control. If there were sufficient public demand for demarchy in such areas as health and education the politicians might see it as a welcome way out of an insoluble tangle of problems. The great advantage that demarchical bodies have over elected ones in areas where there are highly entrenched and active interest groups is that the demarchs are much less vulnerable to pressure groups. They do not have to worry about re-election or party funds or exchanging favours. They can act as independent judges assessing the merits of proposals. They are thus likely to be able to work at a local level and on a relatively small scale while enjoying the relative freedom from local pressure groups that is the great advantage enjoyed by centralized authority. On the other hand they can avoid the disadvantages of centralized authority, namely excessive inflexibility and proliferation of bureaucracy.

There is another very fruitful area where demarchic practices could be introduced immediately without any great upset of existing social relations. In most countries there is already a very large range of authorities called 'quangos', quasi-non-governmental organizations. These are committees appointed by government but with some degree of independence from government in their operations, which range from giving advice to running public enterprises such as airlines or ports. These authorities are often a facade meant to camouflage what really happens by giving the appearance of outside supervision of the bureaucracy. They often provide opportunities for patronage and rewards to loyal supporters. Sometimes they provide alibis for government and sometimes they perform substantial functions. Their proliferation, however, is evidence of the public pressure for governmental accountability. If only there were sufficient pressure governments might be forced to constitute many of these quangos on a demarchical basis. Over time such bodies would be likely to gain in prestige and independence if they worked as they are supposed to in the theory of demarchy. Once it was rolling the movement towards demarchy might accelerate rapidly.

III   DEMARCHY OUTSIDE GOVERNMENT

It is no part of my thesis that demarchic forms are appropriate for every kind and size of organization. Many organizations will find other means of decision-making appropriate. There could still be an important role for political parties in a demarchical regime. They would attempt to mobilize pressure on a variety of authorities so as to produce a coherent shift of overall policy in a certain direction. They would try to stimulate their members to take an active interest in the political process, and particularly to challenge the formulas of representation and the scope and limits of authorities, whenever it was in their interest to do so. Some parties might be closely knit pressure groups demanding strict adherance to a programme. These would tend to have a very centralized form of organization. Others might be broadly based movements devoted to pervasive and open-ended concerns about such matters as the environment or the position of women in society. These might be organized demarchically.

An especially important area where demarchic organizations might prove valuable is trade-union activity. The trade unions could play a crucial constructive role in the restructuring of society if only they could represent collectively the broad interests of the working class. The obstacles to their doing so are mainly clashes of interest between various sectors of the working class, industry against industry and trade against trade, inhibiting the formation of any authorities that can pursue long-term class goals effectively. The unions for the most part avoid facing up to these conflicts of interest by addressing all their demands to employers or government and leaving the sorting out of incompatible demands to those authorities or to the blind interplay of market and political forces. Existing forms of union organizations cannot cope with these problems. Large unions are open to all the disabilities that are produced by electoral politics and bureaucracy. Small unions lack the resources to engage with the wider issues in which workers are involved.

The scope of union activities could be vastly enlarged without bureaucratic centralization if numerous specialized bodies were set up on a demarchical base by the unions themselves. For example, there might be a system of tribunals to deal with demarcation disputes, to restructure union organizations in the light of technological and demographic change, to settle conflicts about relativities of pay between workers and so on. Various broadly based specialized agencies might investigate and develop programmes to deal with pervasive problems such as sexism and racial discrimination, marginal forms of labour, and so on. Other bodies would organize pension funds and make investments in worker-managed enterprises, gradually transforming the relations of workers to capital.

The importance of workers taking the initiative in restructuring their situation can hardly be overestimated. The key theses of revolutionary socialism, that the emancipation of the working class must be the work of the class itself, and that the existing forms of government must be smashed and replaced by better ones, are of undiminished importance. What is missing from the strategy I have outlined is the period of the dictatorship of the proletariat. That doctrine has always been in strong tension with the doctrine of the self-emancipation of the proletariat, since it has always been clear that there is a danger of the dictatorship of the proletariat turning into a dictatorship over the proletariat. If my arguments about electoral democracy and voting are correct this transformation is not just a danger that can be averted by resolute action. It is virtually inevitable. The consequence of abandoning the dictatorship of the proletariat is to be forced to abandon the perspective of traditional political revolutionary action – the more or less violent seizure of state power. But sudden revolution became part of the doctrine simply because it was the standard nineteenth-century form of radical action. The alternatives, parliamentary politics or utopian experiments, were seen correctly as ineffectual or counter-productive, except for limited intermediate purposes. My argument is that these are not the only alternatives.

IV   OBJECTIONS TO DEMARCHY

Incompetence

At the lowest levels in a demarchy the people who gain power are self-nominated as candidates and are selected for office by sampling procedures that take account only of their possessing characteristics that make them representative of some group affected by the decisions that that office takes. There is no test of competence. So many quite incompetent people will nominate, with as good a chance of selection as the most competent.

Imposing any particular tests of competence would immediately make the sample less representative. Such tests would almost inevitably emphasize formal qualifications, which are often irrelevant and often the means by which privileged groups maintain their power.

There are two kinds of incompetence. The worse is the sort of stupidity that may be quite pervasive in a person's character. But that is relatively infrequent. If the members of a committee dealing with relatively local and down to earth questions about specific goods were a reasonable sample of the community in terms of ability and character, there is no reason to doubt that they could handle them. Most of the people who now deal with these problems are fairly ordinary in these respects. Moreover, as every academic should know, high theoretical capacities do not correlate strongly with practical good sense.

The other sort of incompetence relates to specific tasks that require particular knowledge, skill or other qualities. I have argued that it would be worthwhile for people to gain knowledge in an area if they had a chance of having a significant say in it. Moreover, since demarchic bodies would be specialized, it would be much easier for the decision-makers to 'do their homework' than it is in present elected bodies, which normally have to face a wide variety of unconnected decisions about most of which they can know almost nothing.

As for skills, the strengths that are needed are those of assessing evidence, negotiating compromises and making decisions. These are not technical skills. They demand a certain intelligence, and also a certain character, which are normally developed by people who take an active part in the ordinary affairs of life rather than just drifting through it. It seems fair to expect that the people who take an interest in public affairs will come predominantly from among those who are active negotiators in their everyday lives.

A committee does not have to consist of uniformly competent people, particularly if its role is largely adjudication and supervision. Very often a few enthusiastic and able people make the running, and come up with the new ideas, the decisive arguments, the critical questions and the constructive compromises. The advantages of giving these people their opportunities seem to outweigh the probability that now and then there will be grossly incompetent committees.

Expert dominance

It is possible that the reckless or incompetent may ignore expert advice. It is also possible that ordinary modest citizens may be 'snowed' by the experts, or that committees may contain too many experts. Overrepresentation, of course, is a matter of the sampling procedures adopted, and should be corrected by appeals to arbitrating bodies to adjust these formulas. Being overimpressed by experts is now a relatively rare affliction. Notoriously, they differ quite disconcertingly. In any case, it is very easy to institute requirements for relatively wide opportunities for comment before decisions are taken in most cases.

Bureaucratic power

It is probably not so much the expert consultant that people who fear experts are worried about but the entrenched expert, and especially the bureaucratic experts who now determine so much of the agenda, the advice and the options of politicians. Demarchy would break down these positions of power by removing centralization. There would be many little bureaucracies, each under much more intimate and interested surveillance than our present bureaucracies, even at the local level. It is very difficult to imagine life without the state, but if it is possible the problem of bureaucracy should be greatly diminished.

It would be possible to go a very long way towards getting rid of bureaucracy almost entirely, if most of the implementation of demarchic decisions was contracted out to various firms who would compete for the business. The main difficulty in doing so at present is that letting contracts is a notorious source of corruption in both bureaucrats and politicians. However, this corruption depends on three main conditions: secrecy, a network of reciprocal favours and specific kinds of power. All of these could easily be abolished under demarchy. The key in each case is to deprofessionalize power. Once the people already in power have no control over who their colleagues are going to be they will not be able to enforce secrecy. The members of demarchic bodies get to their positions not through networks of party and bureaucracy but by lottery. The hoards of favours owed and expected, of loyalty to an organization and of long-term career prospects have no hold over them. So it is most unlikely that overt bribery could be hidden or that the subtler forms of careerist corruption could be maintained.

Accountability

Demarchic bodies would not be accountable, because they would not be eligible for reappointment. Within the bounds of criminal law they could do what they liked, and suffer no consequences of their actions. This is, perhaps, the central objection to demarchy. The answer is inevitably complex.

First, if the people who make a certain decision are statistically representative of those affected by it, then if it is a bad decision they are likely to be at least as badly affected by it as anybody else.

Secondly, even in our present political structures and bureaucracies the main way by which accountability is enforced in regard to specific decisions is simply the force of public opinion. Those who make decisions have to give reasons for them. Nobody wants to appear autocratic, eccentric or stupid. Whether this force of public opinion is in fact adequate is largely a matter of how open proceedings are, how independent the communications media can be and how much people care. In a demarchy all these factors might be expected to be very strong.

Thirdly, there is a regular turnover of the members of a demarchy, and anybody who is concerned about the way a committee behaves has as good a chance as anybody else of joining it. So the reaction to arbitrary behaviour on the part of a committee would normally be a rash of nominations from people who objected to that kind of behaviour. The situation would be self-correcting.

Fourthly, in most large matters a committee would need funds from higher bodies, and these could hold it accountable for the ways in which those funds were used. Similarly, as I have repeatedly emphasized, specialized demarchic bodies would be interdependent with other demarchic bodies which would withhold co-operation in improper actions, especially those that affected them in some way.

Finally, those who behaved irresponsibly or unresponsively as representatives on lower-order bodies would not be likely to be nominated by their peers as suitable for higher things. If they were ambitious this would constitute a sanction. In any case it would limit the damage they could do.

Conflict or harmony

One question that is often asked about demarchy is, Does it rest on a conflict model or harmony model of society? There is often a presumption behind the question that it presupposes harmony and is therefore hopelessly utopian. In fact the assumption is that society is full of a variety of conflicting interests, but not mortally antagonistic interests.

It is crucial to note, however, that it does not make any claim that present society is fundamentally one in which the dominant problems are of the prisoner's dilemma kind, that is, situations where each party pursuing its own interest without regard to other parties is likely to lead to a worse situation than could be achieved by co-operation. It may well be that Marx is right. The structure of capitalist society may be irremediably conflictual. I believe that it is, and that demarchic control of the major productive enterprises is necessary. How that might be brought about is another question. What I am arguing is that, if it were, the resultant society would be largely free of degenerating conflicts of pervasive and powerful significance.

As for present tactics, my thesis is that it is necessary to establish in the present society instances of the practices and procedures that are appropriate to a post-revolutionary society. To those who believe that capitalist society is redeemable once the market is given a fair trial, the problem of public goods is crucial, and demarchy offers some prospect of supplying them in a way that undermines rather than reinforces state power. Those who persist in the illusion that 'democratic centralism' as Lenin envisaged it is viable might at least consider whether demarchy might not prove less dangerous in practice.

The truth is that it is extremely unlikely that any single model of 'society' is appropriate. There are hosts of different kinds and levels of relationships involving very different patterns of power, interdependence, need, action and opportunity. To adapt demarchic principles and practices to each of these is an exercise I leave to the reader's imagination.

Conservative fears

People of conservative inclinations are inclined to criticize demarchy on the ground that those who volunteer are likely to be the sort of people who are at present radical political activists. A formula that selects people according to background could well result in a group being selected that, in spite of their diverse backgrounds, were primarily representative of political views very untypical of those they were supposed to represent. This does sometimes happen even in electoral contests where the electorate is apathetic and typical members of the electorate do not run for office.

The first answer to this objection is that in a system of choice by lot it is very much easier to stand for office. The very daunting problems of campaigning, buying support and facing all the unpleasantness of the electoral struggle are eliminated. So many people who are not willing or able to go through that ordeal could and probably would stand. The electoral process is more likely to eliminate ordinary people than the choice by lot. If there is a much wider and better informed and more detailed participation in political life, the standard of debate will improve, frustrations will be diminished and sweeping half-truths will have much less appeal. Granted that in an electoral system those between whom one must choose are not a representative sample in any case, the question comes down to this, Which system offers the better chance of controlling the unrepresentative tendencies of representatives?

Radical fears

Before attempting to answer that question, it is instructive to look at the fear that radicals tend to have that demarchy would lead to conservative government, because the average person is conservative. It is minorities that bring changes in society, for better or for worse. Only minorities can lead people from routine acceptance of what is to a vision of what might be. That is beyond dispute, but the minorities in question may be very different minorities in different contexts. It is not at all uncommon to find people who are generally conservative having radical views about specific issues and people who are mostly progressive finding themselves in a conservative position on some matters. Very often those areas in which their views are out of harmony with their overall bias are areas in which they have a special interest or experience. They have formed an independent judgement and not gone along with the received opinions of their socio-political group.

It is very probable that it is just in those areas where they have some experience and some strongly held personal views that people are most likely to want to hold office. So the sample chosen from a set of volunteers is likely to contain many people who are not representative of unreflective stereo-types, whether conservative or radical. They are likely to be a minority in their degree of concern about the issues and their willingness to envisage solutions that certainly would not be chosen by most people who are not so strongly affected by those issues. It is very striking how easily even those who are in principle in favour of reformist, activist politics repress concerns that do not touch their experience. Often they simply say that there are many more important issues and that time should not be wasted on peripheral matters. The great virtue of demarchy in this respect is that it abolishes the distinction between centre and periphery. Every matter is dealt with in specific terms, not in terms of generalities that cannot reflect its importance to those involved.

Representing interests

The response to the radical's fears is not in conflict with the response to the conservative's fears. What I am suggesting is that neither unreflecting conservatism nor unreflecting radical-ism is likely to be dominant in a group of people who are motivated to volunteer for this body rather than some other by their different experiences, hopes and fears about the specific issues *this* body faces. Of course, on balance, these people will also be people with much clearer and stronger overall political views and aspirations than most of those they represent. But it is reasonable to assume that they tend to exhibit the range of views that their less reflective and inter-ested peers would have if they had more stimulus to think about these questions. So, if people's interests are what they would choose if they had full understanding of their situation,

choosing one's sample from the more reflective and concerned members of the various interest groups is likely to give
a sample that tends to represent real interests rather than un-
critical first thoughts or received opinions.

This means accepting a certain degree of what might be
considered paternalism by those who want democracy to be a
matter of instant responsiveness to people's present desires. It
is not likely to appeal to the spirit of the chant 'When do we
want it? Now!' But all of us who are in the least critical of
our own impulses and acknowledge the dangers of myopia and
inertia will prefer that our reflective selves rather than our
present selves will be what count in public decision-making.
Certainly we should by and large prefer that other people's
reflective selves prevail rather than their impulses and prejudices that take no account of our point of view or completely
misunderstand it.

In some particularly difficult matters we might even prefer
a decision about conflicting interests to be taken by a group
that had experience of a similar conflict but in a different
area. For example, in the classical conflicts about locating
airports it might be very difficult to arrive at an acceptable
formula comprising all those groups affected by the question,
and it might be feared that the representatives would not
attempt to arrive at an optimal solution but simply at the one
that best suited the majority of those who happened to be
selected. In such a case it might be sensible to turn the decision over to a jury of people from another city whose backgrounds matched those of the people affected in the city
where the decision had to be made. In other words, it would
be rational to accept a representation that was likely to produce optimal solutions even at the cost of immediacy of
representation. In the long run, in a fair political process, one
would be more likely to secure one's interests by agreeing to
procedures designed to produce optimal solutions than by
procedures designed to ensure that each group got an equal
chance to have its way.

Experimentation

Such a convergence towards a representation of interests could be expected only in the long run. In the short run, it might well be the case that there were great divergences between what various decision-making bodies in cognate areas decided, and between most of these decisions and the majority view in the corresponding constituencies. In part this is to be expected because the majority views are likely to be inconsistent or impractical in so far as they go beyond mere acceptance of the way things are. But a good deal of the divergence will also come from the fact that different directions of change may be chosen. There are often open choices where what will appear best is partly a matter of what establishes itself as new and interesting. What we will prefer is not always predetermined by our present preferences. It depends on the ways in which we, our experience, our ideas, our situation, our relationships and the people we are involved with, change in the process of bringing about some new state of affairs.

In such cases there is no determinate interest to which a series of states of affairs might approximate ever more closely. If we have any overriding interest it is that the range of possibilities open to us should be expanded. We may be able to participate concretely only in one definite disjunct of a set of possibilities, but we may still be enriched by sharing in the experience of others who have chosen other possibilities. So we travel to get some experience as observers of what it is like to live differently from the way we live. None is clearly right. To attempt to reduce the variety to some unitary optimum would be stupid. The inherent problem with any planning based on needs is just that it is utterly incapable of taking account of this open-ended and self-fuelling development of needs. The flexibility of demarchy makes it ideally suited to cope with these problems. At the same time it can avoid the dangers of leaving things to the market, since it can feed into the market prices of goods considerations that the market itself cannot register.

Variety

The impersonal criteria of both government and capitalist bureaucracy inexorably tend to impose uniformity on the solutions given to our problems, in the name of economy of administration and production. Decisions are reduced to matters of routine application of procedures. This inherent tendency of large organizations is reinforced by the dispersion and homogenization of their clienteles. The amount of influence any consumer or small group of consumers has over the policies of these organizations is so small that consumer preferences are not strongly voiced. There is no forum for discussion of possibilities and alternatives, so most consumers do not know about such things. By and large they merely react to the alternatives offered to them, since it requires very great effort to do otherwise and there is little hope of success.

By contrast, if government administration and productive resources were in the hands of decentralized agencies representing informed and interested consumers it is to be expected that a great variety of possibilities would be explored. Many of these, as we have seen, would not be chosen by the people affected if they were polled directly. What I am postulating, however, is that a situation rich in variety would be more acceptable to most people than one of a narrow range of variation, even if much of this variety is produced by decisions that do not represent the opinions of those affected by the decisions at the time. If our long-term desire for variety is to be satisfied our short-term desires must often be overridden, since our short-term desires are often uninformed, unimaginative and cautious.

Control

The question remains, can the unrepresentative tendencies of ostensibly representative bodies be controlled under demarchy? If we say that these bodies not only may but ought often do things that are not in accord with the opinion of the majority of those they represent, where do we draw the line and how do we enforce it? The basic answer is by public debate. We are entering an era in which much more informed debate about public issues is becoming possible. In particular, the development of cost-benefit analyses made possible by the use of computer models is potentially of great importance. It is now possible to produce quite easily complex evaluations that show how costs and benefits vary as assumptions are varied in different combinations, to compare different models of the same situation and explore alternatives much more clearly.

People without any special analytical or mathematical skill can examine these possibilities if they are given access to the right facilities. When we are dealing with specific costs and benefits of particular concrete proposals, even if there is considerable disagreement about the weighting attached to various costs or benefits or about the likelihood of certain assumptions approximating to the facts, the consequences of these differences become much more definite. There is much less place for the sort of vague argument about what might happen, based on vague fears and unspecified assumptions, that has so often prevailed in the past. People are going to expect that anybody who claims to make a rational decision will make quite explicit what their assumptions and preferences are. The more specific the projects under evaluation the more likely it is that we are going to be able to make these requirements stick. It will be easier to force complete disclosure of information and of the rationale of decisions by provisions for prosecution for non-disclosure if necessary. But more importantly the ability of a large number of people to make good use of what is disclosed will be increased immeasurably.

The decisions made will still represent definite choices of assumptions and values, and the results will vary accordingly. But for the most part silly decisions should be eliminated.

The decisions should represent at least genuine possibilities that have sound attractions even if they are very often mistaken. The major hope of personal gain for those who actually take the decision will be the hope of being vindicated by the outcome of one's choices. In such circumstances decision-makers will surely heed any considerations that show that their projects are likely to fail. Moreover, they will be watched continually by their predecessors, especially if they overturn their decisions, and by those who aspire to be selected but have so far missed out. There will be many voluntary groups proposing schemes, questioning decisions and agitating for new priorities. A committee whose authority rests not on force but on public acceptance will have to make a good showing of meeting all the arguments that are relevant to its decisions.

Responsibilities

There remains a good deal of vagueness about what kind of responsibilities demarchic bodies have. In many contexts the role of decision-making bodies may be a judicial one of deciding between conflicting proposals rather than initiating any itself. In other contexts the responsibility of the governing bodies will be that of supervising an expert organization of a permanent kind. In others it may be a matter of hiring professionals on special limited contracts, of allocating resources to voluntary organizations, of organizing co-operation between different agencies and so on. Often the same objective may be attainable in different ways, for example by a body setting up its own organization or by hiring outside organizations to do it. In each case the specific responsibilities that flow from a particular objective and particular procedure for attaining it will be different. The kinds of skill, information and answerability will differ.

The judicial approach will emphasize impartiality, care in evaluation and justifications of decision. The executive approach will emphasize efficiency, effectiveness and sound design. Choice between experts will be justified in terms of conceptions of the task, ways of keeping the experts responsive to public needs and sound evaluation of their performance. As each body would have a great deal of discretion about its mode of operation there could be no uniform way of evaluating them. The evaluation of each would have to be in terms of the soundness of its choice of approach to its problem and the competence of its performance in its self-determined task. The limits within which it can determine its own task will, however, be set by prevailing opinion.

Efficiency

This flexibility might contribute to a certain efficiency and effectiveness at the micro-level at the cost of a substantial loss of efficiency and effectiveness in the overall balance of the political economy. Breaking up conglomerates into specific task teams and giving those teams a free rein might produce much better decisions in most specific cases than a large bureaucratic organization with its rules, its entrenched procedures and its organizational inertia could normally produce. But it is clear that a great deal of brain-power, emotional investment and information processing has to go into making the system work well. It is by no means clear, the objector may allege, that it is worth sacrificing the economies of scale in decision-making and in production and incurring the costs of pervasive decentralized supervision.

The answer to this objection is, I believe, crucial. In part it harks back to questioning the efficiency of large-scale organizations, in part it pleads that advances in handling information greatly reduce the cost of decentralized control, but above all it denies that most of the work involved is properly reckoned as a cost.

To take the first point first, there is no doubt that large-scale organizations can and do achieve great economies in handling sheer quantities either of information or of materials, at the cost of a great deal of standardization. In particular, information has to be processed in terms of clearly defined categories, measures and procedures if the result is to have any validity. It is a common complaint that a bureaucracy generates an enormous amount of information of very limited relevance, because of the narrowness of its base, the crudeness of its metrics and the limitations of the procedures used to process it. We can have a lot of information about our society if we are prepared to shape our lives to the requirements of the information-gathering machines. Similarly, we can have what we like very cheaply if we are prepared to adjust our preferences to what the productive machine is geared to turn out.

There is some reason to think, however, that advances in automatic controls and in data processing have tended to undercut the technical advantages of large-scale units. Modern multi-purpose programmable machines are not tied to a single operation as earlier automatic machines were. So small runs of specialized products become quite feasible simply by varying a programme. Uniformity is not technologically favoured to anything like the same extent as before. Similarly, smaller plants are possible because the overheads of complex control mechanisms are being reduced rapidly as such equipment becomes cheap and the expertise needed to handle it becomes less and less esoteric.

Similarly with information retrieval and processing. It is now possible to have very powerful programmes constructed, quite cheaply, that can be used on cheap computers, to gather and use a range of information that only the largest organizations could afford until quite recently. The development of computer technique has put these programmes at the disposal of people who are much less skilled than was previously necessary, and no doubt the trend in this direction will continue.

Participation

Even if the cost in time, effort and information of running a system of decentralized decision-making were to prove considerably greater than for centralized systems, that cost should not count against demarchy if all the benefits are considered. The most assured of these is probably the likelihood of a varied and interesting society full of varied possibilities. If my contention that demarchy can lead to the elimination of the state proved correct, the cost would be worth paying many times over. Even in the short run the smallest hope of getting rid of the state must count for a good deal, granted the virtually infinite dangers inherent in the state system. These are benefits for everybody.

Many people will find a much more personal benefit in the opportunity of participating significantly in public life on conditions that they can easily meet. People are prepared to pay quite heavily for the opportunity to have interesting work, especially if their basic needs are guaranteed. The notion that everybody should have an active say in everything that affects them is utterly impracticable and pointless. Our capacity for being affected by agencies vastly outweighs our capacity for doing anything significant to control the things that affect us. We can all do a few things well, and what we need in a form of social organization is the opportunity to do some of the things that we can do well, and to be seen to do them well. What demarchy does is give everybody a chance of having a place for a time in a small group where his or her voice can make a real difference deciding about matters of public importance that interest those making the decisions.

Not everybody need feel the need to participate, even though the work of those who do would be suitably compensated and recognized. Society would lack the great 'world-historical' political and military figures of the past. Just as many hanker after the illusions of religions that they can no longer believe in, no doubt many would feel a loss that Napoleons and Bismarcks, Lenins and Hitlers would no longer be possible, that human life would be reduced to human scale and the mythic element relegated to imagination. The easy transcendence of identification with 'great' men and great collective entities would fade. No doubt many would feel that being a big fish in a small pond for a small time is not enough. Fortunately the system could and would continue to work well without such people.

V THE PROMISE OF DEMARCHY

The typical practices of a society, especially those practices that are seen as most effective in achieving the things that are most important to it, influence the character of all the other practices in that society. It is natural to hope that methods that are seen as effective in difficult matters will prove able to deal with other matters as well. We are given to arguments by analogy and the analogies we find convincing are those that are most salient in our experience. Moreover, it is a disreputable tendency of lower-status occupations to borrow the trappings of those to which more importance is attached. In aristocratic societies all kinds of activities aspire to 'a touch of class'. In nineteenth-century Germany the military enjoyed such prestige that professors donned ceremonial swords in place of the traditional clerical garb. What might we hope for if demarchy were to become the dominant mode of public decision-making and the acknowledged paradigm of social rationality?

Beyond the specific benefits that demarchy might bring to a society, it might be hoped that it would promote a spirit of tolerance, rationality and uncontentious equality that would greatly enhance the peacefulness, security and openness of social relationships. People would feel free to differ while remaining within a broad consensus about the way decisions were made and power controlled. No hard and fast global divisions would separate people, no systematically antagonistic relationships cut across social ties. People would have great freedom in moving from group to group. The collective experience would be rich and widely shared. Women and minority groups would be drawn easily and rapidly into public life, and the public sources of racism and sexism would be undercut. The feeling that the problems facing humankind could be solved would be reinstated.

At the same time the meaner and more dangerous kinds of democratic sentiment would be discouraged. It is neither a presupposition nor a likely effect of demarchy that everybody should be regarded as everybody else's equal in every respect. If demarchy invites any person to nominate for base-level public offices without preconditions of any kind, it is on the presumption that the proportion of stupid, malevolent or irresponsible people nominated is in fact statistically likely to be small, and that there will be enough people on a reasonably typical committee with enough of the qualities necessary for the work it has to do. There is no assumption that everybody's opinion has the same claims. At the same time, it recognizes that there are no experts who have the right to pronounce on these matters. They have to be sorted out by a rational social process, a continual debate and testing designed to bring out the best of what each is capable.

The whole tendency of demarchy is to replace the rigid legal electoral and administrative procedures of state democracy, which tend to standardize and atomize people, by flexible, responsive, participatory procedures that permit and foster maximum variety. Even if the amount of work to be done is in aggregate considerably greater under demarchy than in standardized systems, it will mostly be interesting work. The net effect on contemporary advances in computer control is to deskill a great deal of work, as well as eliminate a lot of repetitive work. The same technology can be used to open up different avenues for skill and to eliminate not merely repetitive work but the narrowing of choice to a small range of possibilities. It is clear, however, that these developments will not take place through large organizations, since they need to use technology to standardize operations and simplify the problems of control. Only demarchy avoids the dominance of large organizations and makes the development of alternative technologies possible.

Finally, giving to a much wider range of people, to everybody who wants it, the opportunity to acquire and make significant use of a range of intellectual skills and capacities for co-operating with other people would vastly increase the distribution and quality of those skills in the community. So we might expect a great increase in voluntary organizations and co-operatives of all sorts. The lack of identification with any one community would be compensated by the rich variety of communities to which one would belong and the ease with which new communities could be formed.

In such a community rights to exclude others would be less valued than rights to be included in those groups one wanted to join. In many contexts the free-loader problem would no longer be significant, since much of the work that went in to providing public goods would be rewarding and rewarded. There would be no need for taxation since the costs of public goods would be met mainly by rents on public assets. There would be no opportunity for censorship or secrecy in public affairs. The socialist dream could well be realized without either the unrealistic assumptions that everybody would be co-operative spontaneously or that state coercion to co-operate could be used without danger. The society could afford to ignore those who went their own way as long as it did not involve positive criminal activity.

It would, then, be a society of both freedom from coercion and freedom to do a great many things that most people have never been able to do before, a society of positive freedom. Its main problem would be not that of controlling individuals but of controlling organizations. But since that control is to be exercised primarily from below it does not give rise to any additional apparatus. In the long run social control of organizations is to be maintained by individuals and groups, especially other organizations, refusing to recognize or co-operate with them once they step outside their proper role. These matters will be contested. There will be tension and strife. But granted well-established procedures of arbitration and a spirit of flexibility, problems can be solved and disruptive tendencies contained.

At the same time, the strongest elements of the liberal tradition are maintained. In particular, the individual is in no way a mere element of any organization, and especially not of any total or sovereign organization. Because the trustees of productive resources do not usually engage in production but lease resources to co-operatives and entrepreneurs, there is ample opportunity for initiative and diversity, competition and the fulfilment of individual purposes. What is prevented is the emergence of concentrated power based on ownership of productive resources and exploitation of the economically weak.

Culturally, such a society need not be committed to any ideological orthodoxy of either a collectivist or individualist sort much less to any attempt to subordinate cultural activity to ideological purposes. To the extent that it proved capable of stimulating an awareness of the importance of variety, experiment and innovation it would continue to carry forward some of the most characteristic motifs of bourgeois culture. To the extent that variety and experiment were seen as something done not against social pressure but in an atmosphere of co-operative exploration of the possibilities open to us it might transcend the narcissism of much of our present thinking and feeling.

Demarchy is a practical proposal which is compatible with a wide variety of philosophical conceptions. Nevertheless there are many that it excludes and some that fit closely with it. It fits most naturally with a fairly complex version of historical materialism that emphasizes the importance of relatively 'material' factors, technology, forms of power and organization, as constraints on and opportunities for collective action. Human beings have not made their own history by conscious design, nor is it likely that they will ever have the knowledge and organization necessary to do so in every respect. It is not even desirable, perhaps, that they should. Facing the challenge of the unexpected will always be both inevitable and a vital source of renewal and transcendence. We shall always need to struggle to conserve what we have and to realize our potential in new ways.

Demarchy emerges at the present moment as an historically specific response to the problems and possibilities that have emerged from our present productive and organizational technology and the dissatisfaction and aspirations that are connected with them. It is the form of organization appropriate to a very complex society that generates a host of structures of interests and possibilities. It offers a way in which these might be fulfilled with the maximum diversity in unity that is practically possible. But it rests on no assumption that any global, overriding force, either ideal or material, ensures its triumph. If it comes about it will be because the old order is increasingly incapable of handling the problems it itself generates, and because substantial social forces struggle for it and against the forces that resist it. The forms that struggle will take are largely unpredictable. The concrete sites and issues on which struggle will arise are even less predictable. Demarchy is a proposal, not a prediction.

Demarchy makes a radical break with all those traditional political philosophies from the Greeks to the present that have made some geographically circumscribed sovereign community the highest form of social organization. They were right in so far as the material constraints on production and communication made any wider form of organization pointless or repressive or impracticable. In Aristotle's time the alternative to the city state was the military empire. Production was concentrated in small, largely self-sufficient communities, communications of every kind were slow and unreliable. There was no way of establishing democratically controlled community on a wider scale than the polis. Only a military organization could control a global community.

Moreover, as Hegel, that great admirer of the polis, emphasized, the particular community could hold together as an absolute only in the face of its radical opposition to other communities. In the long run the unity and supremacy of the political community over its members and its territory can be affirmed and renewed in practice only in war. War, said Clausewitz, is carrying on politics by violent means, but he might equally have said that politics is simply carrying on war by non-violent means. The only way to get rid of war is to get rid of both the ideal grounds and the organizational bases of all total communities. It is not enough to attempt to limit the power of such communities, since even the most limited state must cling to its ultimate rationale as the monopolist of violence and sovereignty in its territory.

Sovereignty has always had as its function the preservation of existing entitlements to property and power within its territory. It represses those who challenge the existing order which has always been based on various forms of exploitation of people's labour through the control of the resources necessary for human survival and flourishing. Demarchy is an attempt to put those resources in the hands of those who need them in a way that ensures the maximum freedom of action for all. It is an attempt to get beyond the traditional concepts of ownership that have their origins in the private ownership of natural resources without concentrating that ownership in any organization that can use it as a means of exploitation and repression, whether that organization be a small commune, a nation-state or a world government. Provided we can voluntarily keep our members within reasonable bounds, our means of production are now so various and so bountiful that we have the technical capacity to assure to everybody decent conditions of life on the basis of voluntary co-operation suitably rewarded, without the need for centralized repression.

Demarchy does not presuppose the sort of unanimity of moral ideals and material circumstances that egalitarians from

Rousseau to certain anarchists and socialists have thought necessary for a wholly democratic community. Nor does it presuppose an all-embracing rationality such as both Kantian and utilitarian morality envisaged. It provides a way by which each person or group can pursue its own interests and preferences by negotiation, competition and co-operation with others in the context of a network of democratic authorities. Individuals can give effective expression to their needs and aspirations in the multiplicity of material particulars which they influence. The moral unity of the wider community should, like its knowledge, its art and its material prosperity, emerge from the creative efforts of a host of interacting individuals and groups, each attempting to achieve its own distinctive possibilities rather than some illusory totality or legal rationality. The greatest good of the greatest number is not something that can be produced either by centrally planned political action or by mere competition. The rights that matter are to be established, articulated and safeguarded not by some unitary moral or legal system, but in the struggle of individuals and groups to find the best way of resolving their concrete problems.

Demarchy, then, rests on a rejection of most of the salient features of traditional political philosophies, because most of these have incorporated assumptions about economic, military and social realities that are no longer warranted. At the same time it rejects their cognitive pretensions, their restrictive assumptions about rationality, their vacillations between scepticism and dogmatism about what we are and what we can hope for.

Like science and art, the sort of philosophy that demarchy coheres with is open and experimental. What can be remains to be discovered. The process calls for continual, detailed reflection, speculation, evaluation and struggle. We have no assurances of ultimate success, and indeed no clear idea of what would constitute success. The very criteria of success themselves are constantly changing, not arbitrarily, but in the light of new and unforseeable problems. But by the same token we have no reason to think that we must fail. We have only just begun the task of discovery.

Notes

INTRODUCTION

1. For a good critical survey of contemporary theories of democracy see Jack Lively's *Democracy* (Oxford, Basil Blackwell: 1975). My work is much indebted to the works of R. A. Dahl, especially *A Preface to Democratic Theory* (Chicago, University of Chicago Press: 1956); *Polyarchy: Participation and Opposition* (New Haven, Yale University Press: 1971) and *Dilemmas of Pluralist Democracy: Autonomy vs. Control* (New Haven, Yale University Press: 1982). Dahl has coined the useful term 'polyarchy' to designate the regimes we usually call democratic in Western countries.

2. On ancient democracy see M. J. Finley, *Democracy, Ancient and Modern* (London, Chatto and Windus: 1973) and E. S. Stavely, *Greek and Roman Voting and Elections* (London, Thames and Hudson: 1972). All officials other than generals were appointed by lot in Athens, and the business of the assembly was handled and the agenda set by the council of five hundred, again chosen by lot, working through its smaller executive. Another place where appointment by lot was used extensively was in early renaissance Florence. There, however, the proportion of citizens eligible for office was a good deal smaller than in Athens. The reasoning behind the preference for sortition was simple and sound. If people had to choose they would attempt to elect the best candidates. The candidates with upper-class backgrounds would normally appear superior. The result would be rule by upper-class people who engaged in demagogy rather than democracy. British political history nicely illustrates this point. In other Western countries, where

class differences are not so clearly marked and socially respected, the result of elections is a profession stratum of politicians whose class connections are more significant than their origins.

Of course, it has usually been taken for granted that democracy is inferior to rule by the best. The dominant verdict in Western political thought is in favour of electoral aristocracy.

3. 'Demarchy' is an archaic word which Hayek used to describe the view he advocated in *Law, Legislation and Liberty* (3 vols., London, Routledge and Kegan Paul: 1973, 1976, 1979). However, since he did not employ it persistently, it has not passed into current use and I feel justified in attempting to appropriate it.

4. Rousseau still made this assumption about class societies, though not about classless societies, *Social Contract*, Book IV, Chapter 3. To Godwin, however, writing at the end of the eighteenth century, sortition seemed a merely superstitious practice. The point had been lost.

5. The complexities of problems of rational public choice have been studied intensively in recent years. The best survey is that of D. C. Mueller, *Public Coice* (Cambridge Surveys of Economic Literature), (Cambridge, Cambridge University Press: 1979). See also H. Van den Doel, *Democracy and Welfare Economics* (Cambridge, Cambridge University Press: 1978).

6. The great exponent of this doctrine is John Rawls, *A Theory of Justice* (Cambridge, Mass., Harvard University Press: 1971). There is a very large literature on Rawls's work. See particularly N. Daniels, *Reading Rawls* (New York, Basic Books: 1974) and Brian Barry, *The Liberal Theory of Justice* (Chicago, University of Chicago Press: 1974).

7. Like most nineteenth-century radical democrats, Marx placed his faith in measures designed to ensure that the representatives of the electors acted as their delegates. This assumes that the electors arrive at a well-considered verdict on every important question. I shall argue that this is unrealistic and inappropriate. Not everybody should have an equal say on every question. Moreover, the construction of the common good is a matter of negotiation between different interests, and negotiations cannot be carried out effectively in structures of the kind Marx envisaged. In general, Marx underestimated the extent to which

political structures were subject to inherent laws quite as constraining as those governing economic structures. He saw clearly enough the economic absurdities of nineteenth-century populist radicalism but failed to criticize its political prescriptions. It is easy to excuse Marx's oversights in these matters. It is less easy to excuse his followers, who use the lamest of anti-utopian arguments to absolve themselves from thinking about politics beyond immediate issues.

I DEMOCRACY AND THE STATE

1. The problems of social co-operation without the sanction of state power have been discussed by Michael Taylor in *Anarchy and Cooperation* (London, Wiley: 1976), and *Community, Anarchy and Liberty* (Cambridge, Cambridge University Press: 1982). The conditions that constitute community in the relevant sense are discussed in the latter book, especially, pp. 25–32. Taylor accepts, as I do, the general correctness of Mancur Olson's argument in *The Logic of Collective Action* that individuals are unlikely to contribute their property or labour to the production of most public goods without some private incentive, simply because it is so easy to be a 'free-loader'. Where many people are involved the difference any participation makes is minimal. So it is unlikely to have any effect on whether I get the benefit or not. However, Taylor's judicious comments on the application of this thesis are important. See pp. 50–5 of *Community, Anarchy and Liberty*.

2. Many international agencies are already of this kind. If a country did not obey international rules governing aircraft it would be forced to comply by various diplomatic and commercial sanctions brought to bear not only by governments but airlines, travel organizations, insurers and traders. For the most part nation states hinder rather than help this sort of development, bringing in issues of sovereignty, prestige and irrelevant interests to the negotiation stage and interposing barriers to normal processes of enforcement by co-operative action. See the discussion by Evan Luard in his *Socialism without the State*

(London, Macmillan: 1979), especially chapter 10, which is based on long experience with and study of international organizations. For more detail see the same author's *International Agencies: The Emerging Framework of Interdependence* (London, Macmillan: 1976), and the work of D. Mitranny, *The Functional Theory of Politics* (Oxford, Martin Robertson: 1975).

3. The major theorist of this tendency in modern times is Hegel. It depends very much on accepting the historical fact that the state has developed certain functions and pretensions as evidence for a rational necessity underlying that development.

4. See for example Roger Scruton's *The Meaning of Conservatism* (Harmondsworth, Penguin: 1978).

5. The most obvious model for such allocations of resources are the ways in which various foundations, trusts and public authorities make grants to individuals and institutions for such activities as scientific research and the arts. It seems that this system is both more flexible and more effective than a single highly centralized body could be, and probably less wasteful of resources. Superficially, it involves more organizational effort. Similar applications are made to several bodies and examined several times over, and there is a good deal of lobbying to be done, but this can be minimized by co-operation among those bodies.

6. For a good discussion of the voluminous literature see Bob Jessop, *The Capitalist State* (Oxford, Martin Robertson: 1982). For Marx's own work see Hal Draper's *Karl Marx's Theory of Revolution: State and Bureaucracy* (New York, Monthly Review Press: 1977). Marx used the phrase cited in *The Eighteenth Brumaire of Louis Bonaparte.*

7. Michael Foucault, *Surveiller et Punir* (Paris, Gallimard: 1975). Translated edition, *Discipline and Punish* (New York, Partheon: 1977).

8. The theoretical and social bases of these doctrines have been explored by C. B. Macpherson in *The Political Theory of Possessive Individualism* (Oxford, Oxford University Press: 1962) and *The Life and Times of Liberal Democracy* (Oxford, Oxford University Press: 1977).

II DEMOCRACY AND BUREAUCRACY

1. This chapter is very indebted to Andrew Dunsire's *The Execution Process*, vol. I *Implementation in a Bureaucracy*, vol. II *Control in a Bureaucracy* (Oxford, Martin Robertson: 1978). See also E. Kamenka and Alice E. S. Tay, *Bureaucracy* (Melbourne, Edward Arnold: 1979).
2. I am sorry that I have not the space to discuss Branco Horvath's book *The Political Economy of Socialism: A Marxist Social Theory* (Oxford, Martin Robertson: 1982).

III DEMOCRACY AND REPRESENTATION

1. The classical work on voting procedures is Duncan Black's *The Theory of Committees and Elections* (Cambridge, Cambridge University Press: 1958). More recent developments are summarized in D. C. Mueller, *Public Choice* (Cambridge, Cambridge University Press: 1979), which contains an ample bibliography. A great deal of this work is made up of analyses of models where a very small number of voters are involved, as the title of Black's book indicates. Some of the more obvious problems about voting procedures can be handled if alternatives are suitably subdivided and there is a highly developed trading of votes among voters. But this sort of interaction soon becomes too cumbersome and costly once more than a few voters are involved. In general, then, most of this work has interesting applications where relatively small committees are looking for suitable decision procedures, but is not very relevant to mass voting. What it suggests is that the committees in which, in my proposal, decision power on public goods should be vested, might adopt a variety of voting procedures, depending on the sort of problems they had to deal with.
2. See K. J. Arrow, *Social Choice and Individual Values* (New York, Wiley: 1951; rev. edn: 1963). For a lucid presentation of the present state of the question see Mueller, *Public Choice*, p. 184 ff.
3. The best-known advocates of the view that economic analyses should be assessed solely on their predictive power is Milton

Friedman. See his *Essays in Positive Economics* (Chicago, University of Chicago Press: 1953). For a critique of this position see M. Hollis and E. Nell, *Rational Economic Man* (Cambridge, Cambridge University Press: 1975).

4. The terms 'intensional' and 'extensional' are philosophers' jargon. A context is extensional if one can substitute for a name any other name or description that refers to the same thing without affecting the truth of what is said. So, if Tom Jones ran into Bob Hawke he ran into the present prime minister of Australia, or the man standing at the bottom of the steps in front of Parliament House at such and such a time, or the person who satisfies any number of descriptions that pick out the same person. But of course Tom Jones may *know* that he ran into the man standing at the bottom of the steps . . . without knowing he ran into Bob Hawke. Similarly, where preferences are concerned it is very often the case that our preferences are directed towards objects as seen in a certain light rather than as they are 'in themselves'. So the connections, equivalences and differences between objects *qua* objects of preference become extremely complex and incalculable. It used to be thought that these complexities could be handled by psychological theory, the simplest candidate being a hedonist analysis explaining preferences in terms of the ways in which objects cause pleasure and pain. Bentham's utilitarian calculus depended on this assumption. If there were some independent way of measuring pleasure, and if the relations between objects and the pleasures they give were simply causal, such a calculus might work. But in measuring pleasure we fall back on preferences and which gives us pleasure is not the raw object but the object as mediated by our cognitive relations to it.

5. The prisoner's dilemma is a situation in which two prisoners, unable to communicate with each other, are offered incentives to incriminate each other, there being no other evidence against either on the most serious charges. If A incriminates B but is not himself incriminated he will be set free and B severely punished, and symmetrically so for B. If neither incriminates the other both will receive a light sentence. If both are incriminated both will receive a heavy sentence. So if each tries for the best outcome for himself both will achieve the worst.

Only by settling for second best can either hope to avoid the worst if the other acts in his own interest.

This and analogous situations have given rise to a branch of mathematics known as games theory. See R. D. Luce and H. Raiffa, *Games and Decisions* (New York, Wiley: 1957). Many of the most interesting developments concern complex games in which various situations are iterated in diverse patterns. The development of the theory is severely limited by the complications that are introduced once the number of players goes beyond two. Indeed, many not very complex problems appear to have no solution even in principle.

6. Voter behaviour has been extensively studied. There is a recent survey in Iain McLean, *Dealing in Votes* (Oxford, Martin Robertson: 1982). However, I must confess that my assertions in this section are based on everyday knowledge rather than methodical studies. The issue of competence is very difficult to disentangle from policy issues. A politician may be acknowledged to be 'very clever' but still regarded as incompetent because the policies he or she espouses are unsound. Again, the qualities that are seen to be required, particularly in a president or prime minister will be quite different in different situations and under the sway of different mythologies and emotions. Obviously historical, regional, and economic causes affect these things, and there is no way of disentangling the diverse factors and the levels at which they operate, much less quantifying their relative inputs. Recent studies seem to me to have been strongly biased towards showing that the electorate acts rationally. No doubt there will be a reaction towards sociopsychological explanations in the near future.

7. The problems of systems of voting are well brought out in the context of an argument for proportional representation by Victor Bognador (*Multi-party Politics and the Constitution*, Cambridge, Cambridge University Press: 1983).

8. It may well be the case, for example, that a party obtains power by buying the votes of a number of diverse minorities, and proceeds to enact a package of measures that are contrary to a number of significant majority interests. This may well be possible, because the majority interests may be too widely diffused to organize effectively. What the politician is virtually forced

to do is to construct policy packages with an eye to strategically placed parcels of votes. In different systems this has different effects. So, for example, in the US there is much 'pork-barrelling', buying off of powerful local interests. In the UK this is not very significant. On the other hand parties in the UK rely on class loyalty to keep most of their followers faithful and woo the middle ground.

9. So, for example, I may have conflicting interests as a producer and a consumer, or more generally as a person who wants many things but cannot afford them all. It is not desirable that I settle in advance for some one balance between these conflicting interests. That may commit me to a range of consequences I could not foresee. It is far preferable that I be in a position to adjust the balance between my preferences in relation to the relative costs of alternatives as they emerge in the process of interplay with others. That is best achieved by having separate adjustments to each factor, and this is best achieved by my diverse interests each having its own representation. Each representative tries to do the best for a specific interest in the circumstances. If they do their work well the result ought to be a richer totality than would result from trying to meet the average voter's preferences, since very often the problems do not take the form of zero-sum games.

10. I hasten to add that the point of statistical representation is to get a group that is sensitive to the interests of those affected. This does not necessarily mean that it is a micro-model of the relevant community strictly to scale in every respect. In fact I think it is preferable to have a fairly open-textured sampling procedure and rely on statistical variations over time to achieve balance. It is possible, however, to ensure a high probability of representativeness in quite small samples by using formulas to select the sample that score people along very many dimensions. In particular, there is not much difficulty in getting well-constructed samples of users and producers of goods and services. What is much more difficult is to identify and represent suitably those who are directly and indirectly affected by the production and consumption of those things. Assuming that the question of opportunity costs is covered by a process of adjudicating conflicting claims to resources, the problem

comes down more or less to direct effects on others. The crucial question is one of differentiating legitimate from illegitimate grievances. In some cases it is an offence to pull down a tree on one's own property or paint one's own house a different colour without consent of the local authority in the interest of preserving the visual amenity of the neighbourhood. In some circumstances almost anything one does can constitute an affront to other people. What I suggest in this connection is that the formulas by which representatives are chosen should be open to challenge before a tribunal which would change them in those aspects where it considered that the legitimate interests of people affected by decisions were not adequately represented.

11. It would be possible, and, I believe, obviously desirable, for members of committees to be replaced one by one rather than all at one time. Each member coming on to a committee would be inducted gradually into its operations and build up relationships with existing members. There would be a sense of continuity of knowledge and purpose. It would not be possible for a new group to come in together and overturn existing arrangements without understanding them. A person who wanted change would have to build up allies in the committee, rouse public pressure and produce realistic proposals. Such efforts would be more likely to succeed in an atmosphere of constructive discussion than in an ideological confrontation. There would be a very high premium on presenting proposals as optimal for most of those concerned rather than simply as best for one's constituency. In the absence of party discipline there would be no guaranteed support. Different people would need to be won over on each matter. It would pay to be attentive to the needs of others as a matter of general policy.

12. Michael Taylor, *Community, Anarchy and Liberty*, pp. 26–32.

13. John Mackinolty has suggested that most policing and punitive functions could be allocated to citizens in a way similar to jury service or military service.

IV DEMOCRACY AND MARKETS

1. Nevertheless, a case can be made out in many cases for attempting to control undesirable activities by putting a high price on

them that reflects the damage they cause to other people. Thus it is sometimes urged that pollution should be controlled by selling rights to pollute in some defined measure. Some taxes are practically equivalent to deterrents, for example high excise on spirits and tobacco. Again, in some societies many offences that we prohibit absolutely such as murder have been regarded as matters to be adjusted by compensation in much the way we make compensation for negligent damage. There is a great deal to be said for exploring ways in which offenders can be rehabilitated by giving them the opportunity to do something constructive to compensate for the damage they have caused. The problem is to draw a line between buying the right to inflict damage and making compensation that in no way restores what was destroyed. In the latter case the point of the compensation is to express a change of heart.

In general I believe that a demarchy could find much more flexible and apposite ways of dealing with evils than the law as we now have it can countenance.

2. Amartya Sen, *Poverty and Famines* (Oxford, Oxford University Press: 1982).

3. It is difficult to disentangle these questions from questions of elitism and paternalism. No doubt 'high' or 'fine' art and certain kinds of scholarly activity are pretexts for elitist and paternalist pretensions on the part of those who claim to be their rightful custodians. However, the fact remains that, given normal uncertainties, it is not rational for a private entrepreneur to invest money in advanced music, for example, in the hope that it will become classical and have a much greater market over time than current ephemera.

4. This was the classical position defended, among others, by Locke, though Locke also added the title of improving the land by mixing one's labour with it.

5. As does R. Nozick in *Anarchy, State and Utopia* (Oxford, Basil Blackwell: 1974). The whole question of natural rights is marked by a predominance of assertion over argument. Such argument as is offered usually turns on the consequences of acknowledging rights. But if there are any natural rights such arguments are pointless. The matter is further complicated by the notorious differences in meaning that are covered by the word 'right'.

See, for example, the essays, especially that by John Kleinig in *Human Rights*, edited by Eugene Kamenka and Alice Erh-Soon Tay (Melbourne, Edward Arnold: 1978). The proposals put forward in this book about demarchy do not depend on any particular conception of rights. Even if natural property rights of the sort that Nozick seems to believe in exist, there is no good reason for thinking that any existing property right is derived justly from the original occupiers. Certainly on Nozick's own showing hardly anybody in the Americas or Australasia can have sound title to land. For the difficulties in Nozick's position see *Reading Nozick*, edited by Jeffrey Paul (Oxford, Basil Blackwell: 1981).

6. Nobody, of course, can be statistically representative of posterity, but some groups such as parents of young children who may be affected would be reasonably satisfactory representatives, especially if they were not themselves affected. Here, as elsewhere, the point of statistical representation is not to represent the *opinions* of those affected but to get a group of people who are likely to be sensitive to the *interests* involved and motivated to promote them.

7. In that respect a demarchical polity might well be less just than a bureaucratic one, if justice is a matter of equal treatment of similar cases. However, dynamically considered, demarchy would, I believe, tend to produce more substantive social justice, given time. But the very criteria of social justice vary with one's conception of society. See David Miller, *Social Justice* (Oxford, Oxford University Press: 1976) for a lucid analysis of these variations.

8. The most important advocate of the untrammelled market mechanism even as a means of controlling the money supply is F. A. Hayek. See particularly *The Constitution of Liberty* (London, Routledge and Kegan Paul: 1960) and *Law, Legislation and Liberty* (3 vols., London, Routledge and Kegan Paul: 1973, 1976, 1979). My own work is more indebted to that of Hayek than might appear. It can be read as an attempt at an equally radical rethinking of socialism in reply to Hayek's rethinking of liberalism. Hayek's analyses emphasize the importance of risk and challenge in human affairs. So his justifications and analyses of market mechanisms are much more convincing

than those based on traditional models of perfect economic rationality. In this respect and many others Hayek's work has the rare virtue of not sacrificing applicability to the real world to the construction of models whose only virtue is that they make it possible to make neat calculations of what would happen if the model in fact could work in practice. On the other hand, Hayek is not afraid of arguing that certain things ought to be done even when they are so very much against the current as to seem utterly impracticable.

9. Here, as elsewhere, a favourable outcome depends on the independence and integrity of the authorities who have to make the crucial decisions. Clearly the monopoly prices of natural resources, the availability and price of credit and the consequent opportunities for employment demand co-ordinated decisions and some stability of policy. Perhaps, for example, there could be some system of valuation of resources and each authority might be required to guarantee a minimum return to a consolidated fund for purposes of social insurance and then retain free disposition of the rest of its income for approved purposes. Initially such arrangements would be enforced by the state, but gradually they might be the task of a co-ordinating body set up by agreement among the various trustee bodies that shared responsibility for meeting certain needs of some community.

10. Obviously, if these decisions are made by people pursuing some single interest, even if they are in the majority, the result is almost certainly going to be unfair and a cause of conflict. In such matters voting is a singularly crude and inappropriate way of reaching a common conclusion. What is needed are decisions that gradually remove the undesirable features from existing states of affairs, building on, explicating and adding to the best in accepted standards.

Index